Learn Habits of Highly Effective People & How to Increase Self Discipline

Boost Your Personal Development by Habit Stacking, Stop Procrastinating, Become More Disciplined, and Improve Focus Today!

Pamela Hughes

Table of Contents

Table of Contents
Introduction
Chapter 1 – Habits

> The Importance of Habits
> Cornerstone Habits
> Understanding the Habits of People
> Habits in the Scholarly World
> Authoritative Habits
> Down to Earth Applications
> How Habits Work
> How Do Habits Work?
> Yummy. (The Reward).
> Upgrading Habits
> Useful for Business
> Habit Disturbance
> Identifying Your Good Habits
> Basic Steps to Develop Good Habits
>
>> 1. Utilize Perception and Assertions.
>> 2. Settle on the Choice, and After That the Responsibility, to Change.
>> 3. Enroll Support from Family and Companions.
>> 4. Identify the Habit.
>> 5. Find Solid Approaches to Remunerate Yourself.
>> 6. Devise an Arrangement.
>> 7. Find Your Triggers and Deterrents.
>
> Identifying Your Bad Habits
> Identify the Triggers
> Build up a Substitute Arrangement
> Manage the Triggers
> Change the Bigger Example
> Get Underpins
> Backing and Reward Yourself

Use prompts
Be tenacious and tolerant
Consider getting proficient assistance

Chapter 2 – Habits of Highly Effective People

Empowering People
Help Them Reveal Their Zone of Genius.
Give Your Group the Self-Governance to Do It All Alone.
Be a Supplier.
Approach Them What Their Vision Is for Their Vocation or Employment.
Foresight and Focus
Building Strong Relationships
Faith and Commitment
Love and Romance
Analyze Your Passion Level
Sex

- The Amount Sex Are You Having?
- The No-Sex Marriage
- A Prescription for a Better Sex Life
- Discover Two Bits of Paper and Two Pens.
- Remaining Faithful

Ensure Your Relationship

Chapter 3 – Habit Stacking

What is Habit Stacking?
How to Apply Habit Stacking to Your Life

Build up the Habit of Following the Routine
Case of a Productivity Habit Stacking Routine
Managing Habit Stacking Disruptions and Challenges
The Benefits of Habit Stacking
What Is Habit-Stacking?

How Habit-Stacking Works

My Habit-Stacking in Effect
Habit-Stacking Success Tips
Approaches to Habit-Stack Your Morning

Chapter 4 – Self-Discipline

What is Self-Discipline?
An Explanation of Self-Discipline
The Reasons for a Lack of Self-Discipline
What Is Self-Restraint?
Benefits of Self-Discipline

Self-Restraint Benefits and Importance
How Self-Discipline Can Improve Your Life

What Is Self-Control?
The Most Effective Method to Develop Self-Discipline
The Benefits

Fundamentals of Self-Discipline

Commitment

Optimization
Breaking Point Your Consumption of Caffeine Sources
Inhale Your Way to Becoming a Superhuman
Ponder Your Way to Self-Optimization
Emotions
Continue Practicing Your Emotional Regulation Skills
Exercises to Improve Your Self-Discipline

1. Scrub Down Every Morning
2. Reflect for 10 Minutes per Day
3. Start Your Day With 100 Push-Ups or a 1-Mile Run
4. Make Your Bed
5. Dispense with Distractions
6. Stop Complaining

Self-control and Willpower - Your Inner Strength
Develop Willpower and Self Discipline

Conclusion

Introduction

Congratulations on purchasing *Learn Habits of Highly Effective People & How to Increase Self Discipline* and thank you for doing so.

The following chapters will discuss the habits of highly successful people and how you can adapt them to be successful yourself.

There are plenty of books on this subject on the market, thanks again for choosing this one! Every effort was made to ensure it is full of as much useful information as possible, please enjoy!

Chapter 1 – Habits

The Importance of Habits

Habits are the foundation of your prosperity - or possibly your ruin. However, notwithstanding the significance of habits, few individuals think a lot about how they work.

Habits are regularly thought of as bad things such as having a betting habit. Yet, there can be great habits, for example, practicing routinely, making considerate remarks, considering research themes and hitting deadlines some time before due dates.

A habit is something we do normally without intentionally pondering it. It is a programmed mental and behavioral movement. Habits make it feasible for us to get things done without spending over the top mental exertion. They make regular daily existence conceivable - for positive or negative reasons.

Numerous individuals attempt to get out from negative behavior patterns. Abstaining from excessive food intake is the most outstanding model: it is an endeavor to bring an end to the habit of eating excessively or eating inappropriate sorts of diets. Numerous smokers and heavy drinkers might want to get out from under their habits, and there are a lot of people who might want to support them.

At that point there are habits that block your own personal achievements. Mental habits are significant as well. For instance, focusing on aggravating musings is a habit that can prompt constant nervousness.

In the late decades, specialists have turned out to be progressively mindful of the significance of habits, and there is a developing group of discoveries, quite a bit of it arranged to promote: organizations might want to strengthen or change your purchasing habits.

Cornerstone Habits

For those looking for high-yield results, day by day working is the cornerstone habit. Working with a plan each day animates imagination, centers thoughts regarding what should be perused, encourages research arranging, and much else. there is

Understanding the Habits of People

Realizing that a few habits are harming, scientists have looked for the way to evolving habits. What they have found is that basic habits never vanish. If you have smoked, the desire to smoke can never be completely killed. What can occur, however, is a change to the daily schedule or behavior. At the point when the commonplace signal happens, you accomplish something else, for example, bite some gum.

AA gives an elective daily practice. Drunkards, as opposed to going to a bar, go to an AA meeting. This gives a substitution routine, accordingly fulfilling the hankering. Be that as it may, AA includes one more key component into the procedure: conviction. To change habits, individuals need to trust it is conceivable. Pundits of AA are incredulous of the profound summons engaged with the 12 stages yet conviction is important to AA's prosperity. Besides, being in a gathering of devotees makes conviction simpler.

Building up another habit dependent on brief times of day by day working, and doing the work before you are prepared and when you are not propelled, conflicts with profound situated convictions about how to be an effective scientist. Research demonstrates the program works, however, information of the examination may not be sufficient to conquer dug inhabits. A portion of the keys to utilizing the program are believing that it will work - and thusly making an effort not to re-think the procedure - and going to the gathering gatherings to strengthen conviction. For a habit to remain changed, individuals must accept change is conceivable. Furthermore, regularly, that conviction just rises with the assistance of a gathering.

This is equal to a youthful musician or a youthful swimmer entering a preparation program. You have to accept that the normal activities and preparing are getting down to business, and to confide in the instructor or mentor. Later on, when habits are entrenched, a talented entertainer can tweak the preparation.

Habits in the Scholarly World

In classes that we instruct, we only here and there talk about habits. The concentration in many classes is substance and abilities, and maybe mentalities. Be that as it may, imagine a scenario in which habits are increasingly significant. Think about what is required to turn into a remarkable musician. Research on master execution demonstrates the key is "conscious practice." This is a kind of work on including extraordinary focus on the errand while consistently endeavoring to improve, under the direction of a gifted instructor. In the long haul, habits of rehearsing the violin will have more effect than the specific things learned in any exercise. A huge number of long periods of training are expected to turn into a world-class entertainer. Building up a habit for day by day purposeful practice is the most significant thing to be educated for the objective of master execution.

It is begging to be proven wrong precisely which habits are most beneficial for common expressions understudies. Maybe it is composing, talking, basic reasoning or building up an inquisitive personality. Pick whatever objective you like - on the grounds that most classes do next to no to cultivate a progressing habit. Most understudies study just what they need to: they don't build up a learning habit. Most understudies chip away at assignments just as appraisal due dates approach: they don't grow great investigation habits. Most understudies do just what is important to accomplish their ideal imprints: they don't figure out how to stretch themselves as far as possible.

These types of learning would not do a musician much good. They would mean rehearsing just on appointed pieces, rehearsing just barely before a presentation, and not trying to handle the most testing pieces. The typical learning and study habits of most expressions understudies are not the reason for turning into a top entertainer. Procuring aptitudes in learning and continuous purposeful practice are, over the long haul, unmistakably more significant than learning content, composing papers or passing tests.

The equivalent applies to those of us required as educators and specialists. We invest undeniably more energy instructing and inquiring about as per habits we got years or decades back than we do refining or changing useless methods for working. This resembles a typist who perseveres in a since a long time ago settled yet wasteful two-fingered method as opposed to learning another one.

The high-yield composing system is worked around changing the normal habit for glut composing. This habit includes postponing composing until there is a major square of time or an approaching due date and after that spending long anguishing hours on an errand until it is finished. The thought is to supplant the gorging habit with a different one, brief every day composing. Research demonstrates that normal brief composition sessions are unmistakably progressively gainful - and that it tends to be amazingly difficult to change to the new habit.

Colleges as associations are based on examples of gathering behavior and formal methodology that can be analyzed as habits. It is conceivable to change hierarchical habits - however, this is a long way from simple. The potential prizes are colossal.

An aptitude that would be exceedingly significant to people and gatherings is having the option to analyze habits, choose attractive new ones, and continue to change to the new ones.

Authoritative Habits

In the wake of treating the habits of people, we go to associations. There is an intriguing record of how the chain store Target accumulates data about customers to envision what they are probably going to need to purchase, and afterward promote appropriately direct to every person. If their information anticipates that a client is anticipating her first youngster, Target can send promotions proper to each phase of the pregnancy. However, a few moms-to-be are insulted by an organization knowing clearly private realities about their lives, so Target keenly implants the individual significant advertisements among other apparently irregular ones, so the pitch is by all accounts individualized. However, every family unit on a road may get different promotions.

Strikingly, Target's top administration was unsettled about uncovering the organization's methods. This data is gotten from workers, and incorporates, in his notes, the organization's conventional reaction.

Regarding advertising, colleges are tenderfoots contrasted with Target and different organizations utilizing comparable strategies. Envision a college advancement conveyed through a few online life that is inconspicuously custom fitted for every potential understudy's statistic attributes and individual conditions. That, to my brain, is certifiably not an attractive objective. More with regards to the conventional objectives of colleges would instruct, supervision and companion bolster versatile for individual understudies. Some dynamic US universities do this, with every understudy arranging a learning contract with a scholarly consultant. Australian colleges are dreadfully bureaucratized for anything like this to be practical.

Down to Earth Applications

Numerous readers will ask, "So how would I change my negative behavior patterns? How would I quit gorging and start working out? How would I quit tarrying and start dealing with my significant long haul extends?" The issue is, there is no enchantment arrangement. Obviously not – else we would all think about it as of now.

You have to do some handy examination to discover what the signs are for your habits and what activities you can use to supplant your standard behavior. Suppose you take a gander at your email before anything else, and check news stories around the globe, all of which winds up taking two or three hours and derailing from chipping away at your book. Indeed, you have delayed taking a shot at the book for as far back as year. You have to analysis to find the sign for your email habit, and trial with substitution exercises.

It is not as simple as it may appear. Changing habits should be possible, however, it is difficult, as health food nuts and smokers will let you know.

How Habits Work

Did you make another year's goals this year? Or then again more significantly, did you figure out how to stay with it? Possibly you chose to take up running or to eat all the more strongly. Some sort of moderately "minor" lifestyle change.

It may have appeared to be very direct on paper. Something that you thought was inside your compass. Also, it is useful for your wellbeing. Most likely that is sufficient inspiration?

Be that as it may, the issue is, it isn't just about inspiration. It is about habits. Furthermore, that is an entire other ball game. An entirely different neural hardware that you need to break into. Revamp.

Also, this neural habit hardware to you needs to modify-situated in a piece of your cerebrum called the basal ganglia – is hard-wired for automaticity. It is your programmed pilot circuit. The one that approaches its day by day business without you expecting to ponder it. Something that is extraordinarily helpful on one hand as it opens up your intuition time for other increasingly significant contemplations of the day. In any case, inconceivably disappointing then again on the grounds that it makes these habits extremely difficult to change.

How Do Habits Work?

Researchers have identified a "habit cycle" which clarifies how habits work. There are three components to the cycle – a sign, a daily practice, and a reward. Your mind sees a prompt, possibly something in your environment, and this sets off a specific daily practice. An activity or behavior that you do. Taking part in this normal gives you some sort of pleasurable experience. A reward for your cerebrum.

For instance, perhaps your morning course to work takes you past a specific bistro (the sign).

Each time you see the bistro, you go in a purchase an espresso and a (delightful however undesirable) biscuit (the daily schedule).

Yummy. (The Reward).

Rehash throughout the days, weeks ahead and hello presto you have a habit. A habit that is possibly difficult to break. A biscuit and espresso needing that starts the moment you foresee your voyage to work.

Also, it is your basal ganglia which are engaged with connecting your activities with these prizes after some time. It takes over from different pieces of your cerebrum which were associated with the underlying basic leadership procedure to proceed to purchase that first espresso and biscuit.

Also, when it is given over to the basal ganglia, that is the point at which it has quit turning into a "simply this once" sort of activity and rather is making a course for turning into a full-fledged habit. Programmed. Instilled into your neural wiring. Also, happening without appropriate conference with different areas of your cerebrum, for example, your prefrontal cortex, concerning whether this truly is the best strategy.

And this makes habits hard to break.

Upgrading Habits

In any case, one stunt with attempting to get out from under an unfortunate habit is in reality not to attempt to quit doing it. It is to update it.

If you simply stop it, at that point you are forestalling the mind getting the reward it needs. Also, that makes longings which are difficult to disregard. Making you backslide.

Upgrading the habit is an inconspicuous methodology. Less without any weaning period. More gradual steps.

Take the above case of snatching and espresso and (unfortunate) biscuit while in transit to work. You could overhaul the prompt by taking a different course to work. Overhaul the everyday practice by having some espresso before you get down to business, or when you get the chance to work so you don't lift one up (and the related biscuit) while in transit to work. Change the reward, so you incorporate something scrumptious (however more advantageous) for your work area breakfast to make up for the absence of early morning biscuit.

Your body and mind are as yet getting what they need, however in a way that is better for you. Fulfills that New Year's goals which is still pretty much sticking on. What's more, you didn't even truly need to quit any pretense of anything.

Obviously, a few habits are simpler to break than others. What's more, when they include physiological reactions which edge nearer to habit (liquor, nicotine, sugar, caffeine) you are probably going to be in for an extreme ride. Managing the related withdrawal side effects. Certainly not a change that can occur incidentally.

Also, there is no recipe for to what extent it takes individuals to change a habit. A few specialists state it takes 66 days to shape another habit. In any case, it is close to home. Furthermore, it relies upon the habit you are attempting to change. So take the time that you need.

In any case, that is sufficient about close to home habits. Shouldn't something be said about purchaser habits?

Useful for Business

All things considered, habits make shoppers unsurprising. They are amazing drivers of rehash behavior. Also, they happen throughout the day, consistently. Not exactly mind perusing. Be that as it may, the following best thing – behavior perusing.

Habits mean you can work out individuals' examples of behavior. Foresee how they will act later on. Furthermore, plan your items likewise.

Fitting them to the spot, the time and the mentality of the customer you are attempting to speak to. Expanding the probability that they will lock-in. Buy. Sign up.

Habit Disturbance

However, if you are needing to discharge another item into the market which may expect customers to change a habit, you likewise need to think cautiously.

Take the case of the ongoing presentation of in-shower lotions where you need to saturate in the shower, instead of after it. Truly, it is another item that requires a difference inhabit, however, it likewise fits in with a present habit (scrubbing down) so the prompt and the routine are as of now shaped. Furthermore, the reward is possibly more noteworthy by sparing your time and exertion.

Subsequently, it is a generally simple habit change to present. Problematic. Yet, not very problematic.

Yet, be careful. Regardless of whether you figure out how to get individuals to shape another habit you need to recall that the former one isn't eradicated. It is as yet sneaking there out of sight. Trusting that that snapshot of shortcoming will raise its revolting head.

Another item dispatch from a contender enticing your buyers back.

Or on the other hand, a scrumptious new biscuit flavor to attempt.

Identifying Your Good Habits

We, people, are animals of habit, along these lines growing great habits ought to be basic - right! All things considered, not generally. The issue is that we get truly happy with doing things a similar way every single day. We frequently absentmindedly adhere to a day by day schedule without thinking about the outcome or viability of it. Why change?

Tragically, not the majority of our habits are solid, or great. If we are in the habit of returning home after work every day and going after a mixed beverage to unwind as opposed to jumping on the treadmill to release pressure, it will antagonistically influence our wellbeing.

Or then again, if, while staring at the TV at night we will in general nibble on chips and drink soft drink as opposed to chomping on veggies and tasting on organic product juice, it will at last lead to the result of weakness.

If we are in the habit of smoking to assuage pressure/uneasiness, or over-eating, or taking our dissatisfactions out on others, we should perceive these as habits worth changing, or wiping out. So where do we start?

Basic Steps to Develop Good Habits

1. **Utilize Perception and Assertions.**

    Representation and insistences are incredible for coordinating the new habit into your daily practice. While representation is a ground-breaking inspirational instrument and energizer, certifications program the subliminal with the correct outlook for building up another habit. Together they enable you to feel and envision yourself completing the right behaviors making it simpler to receive the new habit. Unquestionably growing great habits is simpler when utilizing perception and confirmations.

2. **Settle on the Choice, and After That the Responsibility, to Change.**

    Obviously, this is more difficult than one might expect. How often have we said to ourselves, "Indeed, I should practice more and eat better. Not to stress, I'll get around to it at some point or another?"

    Lamentably, stalling just makes it harder to change a negative behavior pattern. The more you put off making a move, particularly where wellbeing is concerned, the unhealthier you, or the circumstance, will get. A cognizant responsibility is important in light of the fact that that is the stuff to get the wheels of movement in real life.

3. Enroll Support from Family and Companions.

Tell individuals what you are attempting to achieve. Along these lines, they will comprehend if you need to leave behind the desert or take a stroll as opposed to halting at the bar in transit home. At the point when your companions realize you are not kidding about changing an unfortunate habit into a decent one, not exclusively will they help you steer away from allurements, they will give a shout out to you and give you good help. We as a whole need support in accomplishing our objectives!

4. Identify the Habit.

As referenced, more often than not we are never again aware of our habits, positive or negative, so the main thing we need do is turned out to be mindful. If that hack has been deteriorating, or if we become winded in the wake of strolling up a couple of stairs, all things considered, a negative behavior pattern (smoking, stationary lifestyle), or an absence of a decent habit (work out) is at fault. Perhaps our funds are in disorder, which implies that we've been in the habit for spending more than we acquire, or not rehearsing the great habit of keeping up a financial limit and adhering to it. It is an ideal opportunity to look at our habits!

5. Find Solid Approaches to Remunerate Yourself.

One reason we create numerous negative behavior patterns, in any case, is on the grounds that they make us feel better, regardless of whether it is simply briefly. The experience of inclination great is intended to alleviate or assuage us when we're focused on, discouraged, or out and out unwell. For instance, you may over-eat and feel great while doing it, yet then you feel twice as awful subsequently. The equivalent goes for smoking or drinking excessively. While you are in the demonstration you feel loose and issue free, notwithstanding, thereafter you feel regret and promise to stop - soon.

6. Devise an Arrangement.

Benjamin Franklin had an incredible arrangement for defeating his negative behavior patterns and supplanting them with great ones. He built up a procedure whereby he recorded 13 ethics he felt were significant in his life and afterward continued to take a shot at them. He concentrated on one excellence for each week overlook great habits a multi-week time frame. Before every week's over he believed he had aced the negative behavior pattern so he continued to the following one the next week.

During this procedure, he kept a diary of his prosperity with ethics. Since a portion of the excellencies encouraged the obtaining of others, he put them in a specific request starting with moderation since "it will, in general, acquire that coolness and clearness of head, which is so fundamental where steady watchfulness was to be kept up."

This will function admirably for any individual who is attempting to build up another great habit - carefulness is in reality expected to ensure you stay with it! After balance he took a shot at quiet since learning could be best acquired "by the utilization of the ears than of the tongue."

7. Find Your Triggers and Deterrents.

If you don't have the foggiest idea what your triggers are, or if you are not ready for the unavoidable impediments, you will set yourself up for disappointment. So as to grow great habits, we should know about what our habits are. We all, in snapshots of shortcoming and defenselessness, need support or a discharge for our disappointments. Going after liquor, drugs, over-eating, or over-curing isn't the appropriate response.

If an undesirable episode happens at work, or an untidy traffic squabble happens in transit home, you need to locate a sound option in contrast to your standard method for managing it. We as a whole have terrible days, however, we need not fall back on unfortunate habits to lighten the pressure. In like manner, we can't give fatigue, a chance to anger, or tension be triggers for unfortunate propensities either. Search for solid methods for managing triggers and snags.

Along these lines, so as to limit tumbling off the wagon and slipping once more into old, negative habits, compensate your self when you have progressed admirably. Treat yourself to another book, a film, a show, or new practice hardware. If you are lacking in real money, visit a companion you haven't seen for some time, go to the midtown craftsmanship exhibition, or appreciate a thin latte.

The brilliant advantage of growing great habits is that in the wake of doing them over and again, they before long become programmed. Anything you accomplish for quite a while and reliably enough, in the end, turns into a habit, and once it does, you never again need to place much exertion into it. Such is the magnificence of growing great habits.

Identifying Your Bad Habits

It is anything but difficult to consider habits falling into highly contrasting classifications — practicing great, gnawing your nails awful. Be that as it may, habits additionally sit on a continuum in our capacity to exercise command over them: Some are mellow, such as removing your shoes and dumping them in the lounge each night; others are moderate, such as having supper before the TV, or drinking an excess of when you go to a gathering; and afterward those that are solid and addictive — like smoking.

Habits become hard to break since they are profoundly wired, by steady redundancy, into our minds. Also, when you add delight to them — like you have with medications or pornography, for instance — the joy focuses of the midbrain get started up too.

In any case, habits are additional examples of behavior and it is the breaking of examples that is simply the way to bringing an end to the habits. As a rule, there is a reasonable trigger to begin the example. Here and there the triggers are enthusiastic — the needing a beverage or cigarette or nail-gnawing driven by pressure. Different occasions the trigger is all the more basically situational and natural: You consider the To be and love seat when you hit the front entryway, and now your mind draws an obvious conclusion, and having supper before the TV on the lounge chair isn't a long ways behind. All the more frequently it is a blend of both — the blend of social tension and the gathering condition prompts your heavier drinking.

In any case, these examples are likewise normally enveloped by bigger ones: This is the place schedules come to run our lives. Here is the place, when you hit the front entryway after work, the dumping the shoes, the getting a lager, the sitting before the TV with supper stream together absent much idea, similarly as your morning work-break consequently prompts you and your companion, Kate, heading outside and visiting while you each have your early in the day cigarette.

By and large, these standard behaviors are developmental savvy and for all intents and purposes great. They shield us from reevaluating the wheel of our day by day lives by settling on an endless number of choices throughout the day, which thus gives us more mind space to consider different things. The drawback of these being routine examples comes when those examples land more in the terrible segment than the great one.

So if you have habits you need to break, here are a few stages to kick you off:

- Characterize the solid behavior you need to change or create

- Getting more exercise or treating your beau better may sound incredible yet they give you to get a handle on onto. You have to take action breaking process by intuition as far as specific, possible behaviors — like not dumping your shoes in the family room however placing them in your wardrobe; not eating before the TV set at the lounge area table; going for a half-hour run five days per week; sending your beau a complimentary book once every day, as opposed to sending him nothing or negative ones. Drill down on the solid.

Identify the Triggers

The icebox might be a sufficient trigger to have you go for the brew once you hit the entryway, similarly as observing the lousy nourishment on the counter will when you get exhausted. Or then again it might be that flash of social tension that wrenches up the drinking when you think about an up and coming occasion with multiple individuals. By identifying your triggers, you have a method for pushing back and not having that autopilot kick in.

In any case, a few people have a difficult time doing this. If this is valid for you, that you have a difficult time realizing what genuinely triggers you, you can work in reverse — see, for instance, when you are longing for a beverage or gnawing your nails, and delayed down and utilize your familiarity with these behaviors sign to ask yourself: What is going on inwardly?

Build up a Substitute Arrangement

Getting out from under habits isn't tied in with halting yet substituting. Here is the place you thought of an arrangement for dealing with the gathering without drinking — getting a mocktail and balancing near to your great companion, as opposed to snatching a beverage and being with stayed with a lot of outsiders.

Manage the Triggers

Since we're needing to break designs, you currently need to take care of the triggers themselves. Here you proactively get the lousy nourishment or brew out the house, or when you understand, while driving home, that you are focused, and you intentionally sit in the vehicle and tune in to music that you like while sitting in the garage, or do a couple of minutes of profound breathing to unwind, instead of consequently walking into the risk zone of the kitchen.

Or on the other hand, if you are worried about your gorging during the evening, plan to bring two treats up to your room at 11 o'clock and resolve not to return down the stairs for the remainder of the night to shield you from winding up meandering around the kitchen all night and veering towards the kitchen. Or on the other hand so as to evade the allurement of web pornography, plan to unplug your PC when you return home and avoid gadgets, and rather settle in with that new book you got for your birthday, or call your mother, all to abstain from falling into your set daily practice.

The key here is mapping this out before that triggers get an opportunity to kick in.

Change the Bigger Example

Here we are extending the setting that encompasses the habit-design. Here you go to the rec center during your mid-day break since you realize the following work is too hard when you are so worn out. Or on the other hand, you understand you don't sit at the lounge area table for supper since it is so stacked down with papers and such, thus you have to begin by both keeping the table clear and preparing the table for supper before you leave for work.

By taking a gander at and changing the bigger example you are really not just making it simpler to handle the center habit, yet are working on practicing your self-discipline on littler, simpler example breaking behaviors. This can add to your feeling of strengthening.

Get Underpins

Get a running mate, or a gathering amigo, or somebody you can call, or an online discussion you can take advantage of when you those desires begin to kick in and you are battling. Converse with your companion about going to get a snappy mug of espresso together as opposed to remaining outside with your cigarettes. Go to AA gatherings.

Backing and Reward Yourself

Sooner or later in your endeavors to bring an end to a habit, you arrive at a point where you go: Why am I trying to battle with this? You feel disheartened, you believe you are sincerely making your life apparently harder and that there is little result.

This is ordinary, the depressed spot simultaneously, and you have to keep your focus on the big picture. In any case, you additionally need to ensure you work in as a result. Here you intentionally pat yourself on the back for eating at the table as opposed to the love seat, despite the fact that you will not promptly feel much improved. You take the cash you would spend on liquor or medications or cigarettes and spare it up to purchase something different you have constantly needed—another outfit, a top of the line small scale get-away. Once more, you sink into having people around you to give a shout out to you and help you understand what you are gaining ground and are in the correct way.

Use prompts

These are suggestions to enable you to break the example by making positive triggers and alarms to keep you on track: Putting your running shoes along the edge of your bed so you see them before anything else, or putting a caution on your telephone to leave for the exercise center, or checking in with yourself and measuring your feeling of anxiety in transit home before it gets excessively high and out of your control.

Be tenacious and tolerant

That is the name of the game, obviously: understanding that it will require some investment for the new cerebrum associations with kick in, for the old mind firings to quiet down, for new examples to supplant the old. Try not to thump yourself for slip-ups or use them as reasons for stopping. Take it one day at the time.

Consider getting proficient assistance

If you have done as well as can be expected and you are as yet battling, think about looking for expert help. This might be a specialist who can recommend prescriptions for the fundamental tension and wretchedness, an advisor who can't just enable you to unwind the sources and drivers of your habits, yet additionally give some relentless help and responsibility.

While all habits are not made similarly, the all-encompassing objective is the equivalent, to be specific you take in charge of your life and being proactive instead of responsive, intentional as opposed to being routine.

Chapter 2 – Habits of Highly Effective People

Empowering People

We live in a culture that is shifting continuously. The sort of pioneer children of post-war America tried to be is different from the sort of pioneer Millennials and Generation X put their focus on.

The shift in authority style has to a great extent been a consequence of the shifting commercial center and what is expected of organizations to be aggressive. Twenty years back, it was about order and control-being unequivocal and definitive. The pioneer of the past was relied upon to have every one of the appropriate responses and guide their workers. Representatives must keep the guidelines, do what they were told, and pay their levy until they were elevated to a place of power.

At this time, satisfaction at work was a pipe dream. You were informed that if you keep your focus on the big picture - power and authority- - at that point, you would be "effective." But I'm not catching that's meaning? In this model, nobody is glad and flourishing. Direction and control make a situation where representatives are famished of self-governance and after that getting alcoholic on power once they get to the highest point of the stepping stool. Everything is out of equalization, and the organization endures.

Be that as it may, presently directing and controlling is clearing a path for an increasingly community-oriented method for driving. The market is requesting advancement at such a quick rate, that unlimited thoughts are required so as to contend. These unlimited thoughts can't just originate from a pioneer; however, they should originate from every other person included.

In this manner, the pith of administration is shifting from instructing everybody, to enabling others to think of the best and most brilliant thoughts that have never been idea of. How at that point do you enable individuals to be their best?

Here are six incredible ways you can start to have business accomplishment by helping your group be their best:

Live the behaviors that you need them to grasp.

Guiding different grown-ups isn't a successful inspiration system. When was the last time being determined what to do made you feel motivated and prepared to roll out genuine improvement? Likely never, in light of the fact that this is the most exceedingly terrible approach to get people to change. You realize what is profoundly viable? Exhibiting the behaviors, activities, and qualities you want to find in others. Nonetheless, this requires duty and order from you, the pioneer. You must be the individual you need your group to be.

Help Them Reveal Their Zone of Genius.

Your Zone of Genius is the crossing point of your inborn intellectual competence and your motivation. Your mental attitude is the manner by which your cerebrum naturally prefers to issue comprehend and process data. Your motivation is connected to what makes satisfaction for you and is associated with your brain research. Make sense of your most noteworthy life challenge-- the one thing that you generally adapt to the situation to help other people with. That is your Zone of Genius. At that point, you have the formula for interminable inspiration when you need it.

Give Your Group the Self-Governance to Do It All Alone.

Don't micromanage- - another inspiration executioner. Give individuals space. I have met endless CEOs that have moved to a Results-Only Work Environment. All CEOs detailed expanded inspiration and dedication. Give your kin more opportunity than you feel good with- - what appears the scariest activity some of the time is the most dominant. Your group will come back with results you can't envision.

Be a Supplier.

In his book Give and Take, Adam Grant takes note of that best individuals provide for others without contemplating receiving anything consequently. When you need to engage others, provide for them. Be liberal, and they will feel associated with you, increased in value by you, and motivated to do likewise.

Approach Them What Their Vision Is for Their Vocation or Employment.

A great many people don't have the foggiest idea of what their vision is for their profession or occupation. The significance of a dream is that it can manage you in snapshots of progress or in venture prioritization. Having your kin know the bearing they need to control themselves improves effectiveness as well as a simple method to guarantee they are figuring out how to inspire themselves.

Keep away from offering your group the responses. Or maybe, express the issue and let them think of the arrangement.

This is tied in with overseeing yourself. We frequently do things unwittingly and after that question why we are not getting the outcomes we need. Watch yourself all the more intently with regard to what you state to your group or others. It is safe to say that you are keeping away from instructing them? You should, yet this isn't simple. We live in a power-hungry society and it is simpler to utilize our capacity muscle, instruct others and use it as a chance to stroke our own personalities. This doesn't, notwithstanding, engage others to be their best.

At the point when individuals feel enabled, they put stock in themselves and their capacity to control their own and expert lives. Engaging others advances positive thinking and a "can-do" soul that completes things—quicker and better. Here are 10 hints for helping other people become all they are fit for being.

Try not to strive to be the focal point of consideration; share the spotlight and gathering achievement. Hoarding the spotlight generally creates disdain, while sharing makes certain to bring gratefulness and appreciation.

Give wholeheartedly of your time and consideration, without anticipating anything consequently. Companions and associates will, thus, feel acknowledged and return your liberality in kind.

Make a special effort to interface with new partners. Visit with them, welcome them out for an espresso; make them feel that they are a welcome, esteemed piece of the group.

Model positive character characteristics you have faith in. Others will pay heed and copy your words and activities.

If you are responsible for a gathering, let everybody know your worth their assessment. Energize the individuals who might be modest to shout out. Try not to put down anybody's commitments, regardless of whether you can't help contradicting those specific ideas.

Listen eagerly. Try not to lose the center when somebody addresses you. Take a gander at them and gesture to show you are following the discussion. This will urge the other individual to keep on sharing their thoughts.

Offer individuals the two most underestimated words in the English language: "much obliged." They show others that you saw their assistance or potentially capacities and are thankful.

Give direct reports of self-governance. Give them a chance to come up with their very own thoughts and answers. Individuals who feel responsible for their decisions more joyful, progressively satisfied—and increasingly beneficial. Act toward others as you would have others act toward you—with benevolence, thought and regard.

Give genuine compliments, regardless of whether you are applauding the nature of somebody's work, their assistance with a task, or another outfit.

Foresight and Focus

What's to come is too imperative to possibly be left to risk. Previously, organizations outlasted individuals. Presently, it is regularly a different way.

Mohist rhetoric can be used to counter the spread of misinformation by government agencies because it offers a basis for 'universal love' and submission to the 'will of Heaven.' Mohist rhetoric is a Chinese philosophy that emphasizes the importance of God (the Lord on High) and universal love is radically changing behavior in society. This philosophy was conceived by Mozi through his teachings, and it emphasizes practicality and equality in society. One of the fundamental aspects of the philosophy is that it emphasizes a meritocratic society that is led by a virtuous monarch and officials who have been appointed on the basis of their abilities to handle the responsibilities rather than social status. The philosophy is particularly critical of the excesses of society, such as the Confucian funeral rites that used a significant amount of funds that would be better spent in society.

This rhetoric can be used to counter the spread of misinformation by government agencies by utilizing the Mohist advice in the selection of appropriate leaders. Mohist rhetoric emphasizes selecting leaders based on their skills and capabilities rather than their background, and this will go a long way in ensuring those in charge of information do not spread misinformation. Similarly, Mohist rhetoric points to the importance of a superior being in society, God; thus, all actions undertaken by a government agency should incorporate the teachings and instructions of God when dispatching information. Thus, all action taken by the government should take into consideration 'the will of Heaven' and ensure that all activities undertaken is per God's laws. Therefore, this paper will provide information on the specific ways that the Mohist rhetoric can be used to counter the spread of misinformation by government agencies.

Mohist reasoning was characterized by specific principles that provided its followers with a basic understanding of how to conduct themselves in society. One of the critical characteristics of Mohist reasoning was that there should be an emphasis on frugality and utility among the population. This means that all the resources in society should be coordinated and used towards advancing the progress of the community and enhancing the welfare of each individual. Therefore, all activities taking place in society should take into consideration the general progress expected for the community without bias.

The condemnation of luxury and waste in society is also another critical characteristic of Mohist reasoning. The principles of this ideology are that luxury in society should not be tolerated, particularly at the expense of the general activities that will promote progress in the community. Individuals in positions of authority should not live their lives in luxury while the rest of the population mires in poverty. In the same light, waste should also not be tolerated because it is necessary to bring together all the resources of the community towards bettering the welfare of each individual. Therefore, luxury and waste are fundamental aspects of the community that must be avoided for the sake of a better tomorrow.

Another important characteristic of Mohist reasoning is a utilitarian approach in the management of the affairs of the community. 'Concerned with the common people, they propelled a utilitarian political-social philosophy, directed towards the material well-being of all. All actions taken in society by figures of authority must recognize the benefits of every member in the community as opposed to single groups of individuals. This means that in a Mohist society, good morals encompass those actions that will be favorable to the majority of people. Therefore, this crucial characteristic of Mohist reasoning provides an emphasis on impartial care for each member of the community regardless of their social status.

Reverence for God (the Lord on High) as another important characteristic of Mohist reasoning that guided the decisions and actions taken by Mohists at the time. The Mohists believed that all life originated from God, and that having reverence and respect for him was the only way society could progress. The Mohists also emphasized worshipping traditional deities and maintaining the importance of a supreme being as being an important aspect of Chinese culture. Therefore, this characteristic enabled each individual to respect each individual on the basis of the same love that God has for everybody.

Mohist reasoning can be used as a tool of argumentation to counter common misinformation tactics found today. First, Mohist reasoning involves the belief that figures of authority in society should be appointed to such posts based on their abilities to get the job done rather than social status. This means that the leaders in society will have gone through extensive screening processes to ensure that they are morally upright individuals trusted by a majority of the public. Therefore, this approach can be used to counter the spread of misinformation by ensuring that there are credible leaders selected by the majority to ensure actions taken by the government work in the best interest of the public.

Similarly, Mohist reasoning can be used to tackle the challenge of misinformation in the present-day world by condemning the luxuries and wastes of society. A luxurious society will be indifferent to the information they receive as long as it does not affect the luxury, and this promotes the spread of misinformation. Also, a wasteful society will be comprised of misinformation because most people will be convinced not to think about the waste that is actually being generated around them. As Chris Fraser has pointed out, drawing distinctions in this way is the functional equivalent, in Mohist thought, of making a judgment or forming a belief. The ability to draw the distinctions correctly is knowledge. Therefore, employing Mohist reasoning to the conduct of life and society to manage luxury and waste in a systematic way will help counter the spread of misinformation associated with these ills of society.

The utilitarian approach of Mohist reasoning can also be used to counter the spread of misinformation by highlighting the fact that all information should benefit every individual. An important characteristic of misinformation is that the action is perpetuated for the benefit of only a few while the majority have to live with a lie. Therefore, a utilitarian approach emphasizes sharing true information with as many people in society as possible with the desired impact being favorable to the members of the community.

Building Strong Relationships

The most significant single fixing in the equation of achievement is realizing how to coexist with individuals. — Theodore Roosevelt

One of the most significant encounters we can have in our lives is the association we have with other individuals. Positive and strong connections will assist us with feeling more advantageous, more joyful, and increasingly happy with our lives. So here are a couple of tips to assist you with developing progressively positive and solid connections in all parts of your life:

Ethics and morals describe the proper ways of governing human behavior that guarantee everybody lives in peace and harmony. Observing the codes of ethics is an integral part of society today because it ensures that there is equity as well as justice. These rules specify the manner in which people should live and interact with one another without any discrimination or favor against other individuals. There are various scopes of ethics and morals that govern how people live with each other and manage the resources around them. The concept of ethics can apply to a different set of individuals in society and the surrounding environment.

Ethically, people should live with respect and jovial regard for one another to ensure that there is no bias. Each person on earth is equal and has the right to share the freedoms of everybody else. This means that behaving in a moral manner does not anger or limit the opportunities of another person in a purposeful way. Instead, there is careful regard for the interests of other individuals as well as the welfare of the entire community. This careful approach towards minding the well being of the surrounding people constitutes ethical behavior.

The laws that govern countries and nations on earth also have a significant influence in shaping the views on ethics and morals. The laws provide definite rules and regulations that determine the manner in which people will interact with one another. The laws are very clear on the activities that have the consideration of being legal or not. Therefore, those individuals who act outside the bounds of the law are liable for punishment because their actions were not ethical. Remaining within the boundaries of the law is essential in ensuring there is a high level of accountability among everybody. This reduces the chances of disharmony and quarrels because everybody has the perception of being on a level field with other people in the community.

Religions that exist in the world are also very influential in shaping the views on morals and ethics. This is because religious teachings provide a basis for the best human behavior and positive activities that assure the best out of everybody. Religion is very strict in providing details about how people should live with one another because it distinguishes good behavior from the bad. Thus, acceptable behavior according to religion is ethical and moral because it does not negatively influence the surrounding society.

The manner in which people interact with the environment is also a significant influence on the views of morals and ethics. It is vital that human beings mind the surrounding environment and ensure its existence for years to come because it is the most ethical action to perform. Preserving the environment is a vital concept because human life firmly depends on the well being of the natural ecosystems. Thus, it is ethical behavior to conserve and manage the environment to ensure its virility in supporting life and being available for future generations, as well.

In line with the subject matter of Prey, there are a number of contrasts as well as comparisons with today's technology. The book by Michael Crichton, Prey, talks about the technological advancements that might shape the earth one day. The plot of the story takes shape through a woman who is working in the nanotechnology department section of her company. She quickly rises to prominence mainly because her husband loses his job and becomes a sit-in partner. Thus, the wife has to focus all her energy on her career in order to support her family and achieve her interests, as well.

Thus, one of the main contrasts of the subject matter of Prey with today's technology is the existence of robots. The storyline talks about the protagonist looking for an appropriate technological strategy to develop the latest machine. Her work is top secret and even her husband has no idea what she is working on. Her isolation in developing this technology causes her husband to believe that she is having an extramarital affair when she is away. But the reality is that the development of this technology does not compare with anything present in today's society, meaning that she needs a lot of time out to develop it.

The development of robots is a dominant feature of the work by Michael Crichton. The story is very futuristic as it provides details of the manufacture and development of these machines and incorporating them in society. This technology currently does not exist in today's world mainly because it is still in its initial stages of development. Thus, this disambiguation provides an insight into the possible future of the world with the incorporation of robots into various operations. This technology has significant advancements that highlight the main differences with today's technology.

In addition to the differences in the level of technology in Crichton's book and today's world, there is a lot of information about genetic engineering. Relatively new to the world of technology, genetic engineering involves altering the genes within different species of animals and human beings to achieve biological balances. Genetic engineering is a sensitive topic because it goes against the norms of society, especially religious opinion. This is because the purposes and processes of genetic engineering have close links to the creation of beings, a concept that only has an association with God and other superior beings.

Thus, the comprehensive explanations about genetic engineering serve to open up a future world where anything might be possible. This obvious difference in the capabilities of human beings in the future highlights the major contrast of Crichton's book with the current technology. The ability to develop and alter genetic material in order to create other beings is a concept that scientists can only dream about in today's world. However, there are moderate introductions of genetic engineering in today's technology, but the levels that Crichton talks about in his novel are far ahead of today's time. This is one of the contrasting issues in Crichton's novel of today's technology and that of the future.

Another essential issue in discussion in the novel is the issues surrounding artificial intelligence. There is a lot of similarity of this technology with the current achievements in today's world. This is because several scientists around the world are already practicing artificial intelligence to induce life and ensure appropriate biological balances. Thus, artificial intelligence usually involves the manual combination of genetic factors in both animals and human beings that leads to life. This technology offers a suitable method of controlling populations within a given region because it offers the ability to add life to the planet.

The book by Michael Crichton offers some similarities as well as differences in the development and application of artificial intelligence. In today's technology, using artificial intelligence for biological factors has a number of disadvantages as well as advantages. There is a lot of room for error because the development of the technology is still ongoing. This means that there is still a lot of room for error as there is the possibility that it will not work. This means that there is still room for improving the current levels of technology surrounding artificial intelligence.

However, according to the descriptions of Michael Crichton in his novel, Prey, the future will hold some of the most significant changes to artificial intelligence. Among the major details in the novel include the accuracy and appropriateness of artificial intelligence in regulating life on earth. As a result of this technology, it is possible for scientists to schedule the creation of human life through appropriate scientific techniques. This futuristic technology is responsible for increasing life manually both in animals and human beings, leaving very little room for error. In addition to the knowledge from genetic engineering and nanotechnology, it is possible for scientists to rapidly create new life in shocking precision.

Therefore, the technological advancements of the future are very different from the current technology in today's world. But according to Crichton's novel, human beings will eventually reach the stage where they played almost the same role as God. His frightening ability to determine the creation of life and the control of several biological factors brings up the issues of ethics and morality. This is because, according to the present world, it is ethical to fully obey God, avoid blasphemy and take up some of his roles, like the creation of life.

Here are also other similarities and differences in the technology within Crichton's novel and today's world. In respect to the additional knowledge human being possess in the creation of life, artificial life soon becomes an issue as there are several beings on Earthborn this way. Artificial life is a controversial issue because lifeforms represent the work of human beings rather than a superior being. Even scientists acknowledge that the origin of life must have been from an external force with superior powers than the ordinary person. Thus, the ability to create life raises a lot of questions and questions the ethical and moral fiber of artificial life.

In addition to the biological focus of enhancing technology, there are significant developments in the field of scientific computing. In the future, computers become more complex and technical to use as they acquire attributes that are closer to the human brain. The power and complexity of these computers allow for their durability because they use alternative energy sources. This means that they offer a larger and better life span than today's technology where only a few computers have the power to match.

One of the significant additions to the technology surrounding computers is a battery with the capability to survive for a very long time. This allows the computer to perform complex operations that bear similarity to the operations of the brain. This raises ethical as well as moral questions in today's world because only God can biologically create a complex organ capable of complex operations.

This perception seems to be at the back foot of Crichton's novel as he goes on to explain the complexity of the evolution of computers. The result of this evolution is a very technical machine that does not correspond to the modern technology in today's world.

The purchasing world and scientific advances in computers is the right approach when seeking to know more about Crichton's technology descriptions. It is appropriate for the individual to do some research into the market as well as the available products. It is one thing knowing the type of watch to buy; it is another thing getting an appropriate dealer to help. Thus, doing early research on the internet about the technology will enable the individual to open up their options. This way, it will be possible to find the right professionals who will sell the right product at a good price.

Some of the main features include the option to come in a digital or the traditional model. This is essential because the market consists of customers with different tastes and preferences, thus drawing relevance on stocking up with several options. The watches have waterproof installations in addition to high power batteries that guarantee the watch remains active for a long period of time. Additionally, another interesting feature of the watch is a classic, leather strap option that allows the user to get the best possible product. These features enhance the watch and enable it to compete strongly within the market.

One of the main advantages of purchasing this watch is its long-lasting battery that enables the watch to remain durable for years. A steady battery ensures that the watch does not stop functioning within a short time. Another advantage of this watch is that it is practical as it can be used by anybody. Its waterproof abilities enable it to be practical for use both in the office as well as manual labor activities. Lastly, purchasing this watch will allow the user to access a one year guarantee that allows them to get their money back if they are not satisfied with the product.

One of the disadvantages of this watch is its relative pricing within the market. In comparison to most other watches within this class, it is pricey and is likely only to attract a few interested customers. In addition to this, its main features and appearance bear resemblance to other products within the market. This means that the consumer has a wide variety of options to select from and can easily look over the novel, Prey. Lastly, the leather option is an additional extra that the customer will have to pay for, meaning that they will spend more money to get the best watch.

Despite the disadvantages, the watch is modern and appealing for the current generation, incorporating the latest changes. In the dark, the watch-hands as well as the figures of the digital watch are luminous and allow it to be used in the darkest scenario. The styling and craft behind the final product makes it beautiful to wear and appealing to onlookers. Therefore, it is a pleasing product to have and likely to improve in value in the future due to its aesthetic appeal. Thus, customers should look no further if they want to fully benefit from the futuristic technological advancements.

Thus, the major ethical discussions and debates surrounding the technological descriptions in Crichton's novel mainly revolve around religious factors. Religion offers a significant basis for developing ethical and moral opinions in today's world, thus offering an excellent description of some of the dilemmas in the book. Religion is very clear and categorical on the origins of human beings and all other life on earth. It specifically states that human beings are the product of the work of God and only He can regulate, end and create new life.

Thus, Crichton's descriptions of artificial life and the complex advancements in the scientific world create ethical dilemmas because most people believe that life comes from a superior being. Therefore, the main ethical issues in discussion, in this case, are the capabilities and expertise of the human being in relation to God. The reader of this novel will find it difficult to believe that human beings will advance to a level where they can regulate life on Earth. This creates a lot of controversy because today's technology s nowhere near achieving these scientific fetes.

The description of the issues surrounding ethics in today's world is that man has a limit towards achieving the success of God. Thus, the constant reference to modern technology that rivals the power of God is the most significant ethical issue in discussion. There is a lot of association of a lack of ethics in the future of the world as a result of the rapid advancements in technology. Therefore, the novel, Prey, offers an insight into the role of technology in determining the fate of human beings in the future world.

Faith and Commitment

Would you be able to recognize a decent relationship? Obviously, no one realizes what truly goes on between any couple, yet many years of scientific examination into adoration, sex and connections have instructed us that various behaviors can foresee when a couple is on strong ground or set out toward harried waters. Great connections don't occur without any forethought. They take responsibility, bargain, pardoning and a large portion of all — exertion. Continue perusing for the most recent in relationship science, fun tests and accommodating tips to enable you to manufacture a more grounded bond with your accomplice.

Love and Romance

Beginning to look all starry eyed at is the simple part. The test for couples is the manner by which to revive the flames of sentiment every now and then and develop the develop, confiding in adoration that is the sign of an enduring relationship.

- What's Your Love Style?

- When you state "I adore you," I'm not catching your meaning?

- Sentimental: Based on energy and sexual fascination

- Closest Friends: Fondness and profound love

- Consistent: Practical sentiments dependent on shared qualities, monetary objectives, religion and so forth.

- Energetic: Feelings evoked by tease or feeling tested

- Possessive: Jealousy and fixation

- Unselfish: Nurturing, consideration, and sacrifice

Specialists have discovered that the adoration we feel in our most dedicated connections is ordinarily a mix of a few different types of affection. In any case, frequently, two individuals in a similar relationship can have altogether different adaptations of how they characterize love. Scientists give the case of a man and lady eating. The server plays with the lady; however, the spouse doesn't appear to notice, and discussions about replacing the oil in her vehicle. The wife is vexed her better half isn't envious. The spouse feels his additional work isn't valued.

What does this have to do with affection? The man and lady each characterize love differently. For him, love is functional and is best appeared by steady motions like vehicle upkeep. For her, affection is possessive, and a desirous reaction by her significant other makes her vibe esteemed.

Understanding what makes your accomplice feel adored can enable you to explore struggle and set sentiment back into your relationship. You and your accomplice can take the Love Style test from Dr. Hatkoff and discover how every one of you characterizes love. If you become familiar with your accomplice inclines toward envy, ensure you see when somebody is playing with that person. If your accomplice is handy in affection, see the numerous little ways the person in question shows love by dealing with regular needs.

Sentimental love has been known as a "characteristic compulsion" since it initiates the mind's reward focus - strikingly the dopamine pathways related to illicit drug use, liquor, and betting. Be that as it may, those equivalent pathways are likewise connected with oddity, vitality, center, learning, inspiration, delight and desiring. No big surprise we feel so empowered and roused when we begin to look all starry eyed at!

Yet, we as a whole realize that sentimental, energetic love blurs somewhat after some time, and (we trust) develops into an increasingly mollified type of submitted love. All things being equal, numerous couples long to revive the flashes of early romance. Be that as it may, is it conceivable?

Explore new territory and different - and ensure you do it together. New encounters enact the cerebrum's reward framework, flooding it with dopamine and norepinephrine. These are similar mind circuits that are lighted in early sentimental love. Regardless of whether you take a ceramics class or go on a wilderness boating trip, initiating your dopamine frameworks while you are as one can help bring back the fervor you felt on your first date. In investigations of couples, Dr. Aron has discovered that accomplices who normally share new encounters report more prominent lifts in conjugal satisfaction than the individuals who just share charming however natural encounters.

Analyze Your Passion Level

The brain research educator Elaine Hatfield has recommended that the adoration we feel right off the bat in a relationship is different than what we feel later. Right off the bat, love is "enthusiastic," which means we have sentiments of exceptional yearning for our mate. Longer-term connections create "companionate love," which can be depicted as a profound friendship, and solid sentiments of duty and closeness.

Where does your relationship arrive on the range of affection? The Passionate Love Scale, created by Dr. Hatfield, of the University of Hawaii, and Susan Sprecher, a brain science and humanism educator at Illinois State University, can enable you to measure the energy level of your relationship. When you see where you stand, you can begin taking a shot at infusing more energy into your association. Note that while the scale is broadly utilized by relationship analysts who study love, the test is in no way, shape or form the last word on the strength of your relationship. Take it for entertainment only and let the inquiries rouse you to converse with your accomplice about enthusiasm. All things considered, no one can really tell where the discussion may lead.

Sex

For most couples, the more sex they have, the more joyful the relationship.

The Amount Sex Are You Having?

How about we start with the uplifting news. Submitted couples truly have more sex than every other person. Try not to trust it? While the facts demonstrate that solitary individuals can amuse you with accounts of insane sexual scenes, recall that solitary individuals additionally experience long droughts. A report in 2017 found that 15 percent of men and 27 percent of ladies revealed they hadn't engaged in sexual relations in the previous year. What's more, 9 percent of men and 18 percent of ladies state they haven't had intercourse in five years. The primary components related to a sexless life are more seasoned age and not being hitched. So whether you are having dedicated or hitched sex once every week, when a month or only six times each year, the truth of the matter is that there is still somebody who might be listening having less sex than you. What's more, if you are one of those individuals NOT having intercourse, this will brighten you up: Americans who are not having intercourse are similarly as glad as their explicitly dynamic partners.

The No-Sex Marriage

For what reason do a few couples sizzle while others fail? Social researchers are reading no-sex relationships for intimations about what can turn out badly seeing someone.

It is evaluated that 15 percent of wedded couples have not had intercourse with their life partner over the most recent a half year to one year. Some sexless relationships began with next to no sex. Others in sexless relationships state labor or an undertaking prompted an easing back and in the end halting of sex. Individuals in sexless relationships are commonly not so much glad but rather more prone to have considered separation than the individuals who have ordinary sex with their mate or submitted accomplice.

If you have a low-sex or no-sex marriage, the most significant advance is to see a specialist. A low sex drive can be the aftereffect of a therapeutic issue (low testosterone, erectile brokenness, menopause, or misery) or it very well may be a reaction of a prescription or treatment. A few researchers estimate that developing the utilization of antidepressants like Prozac and Paxil, which can discourage the sex drive, might contribute an expansion in sexless relationships.

While a few couples in sexless relationships are cheerful, actually the more sex several has, the more joyful they are as one. It is difficult to revive a marriage that has abandoned sex for quite a long time, however, it very well may be finished. If you can't live in a sexless marriage however you need to remain wedded, see a specialist, see an advisor and start conversing with your accomplice.

Here is a portion of the means specialists prescribe to recover a sexless marriage in the room:

- Converse with one another about your wants.
- Have a ton of fun together and share new encounters to remind yourself how you began to look all starry eyed at.
- Clasp hands. Contact. Embrace.

Engage in sexual relations regardless of whether you would prefer not to. Numerous couples find that if they constrain themselves to engage in sexual relations, soon it doesn't move toward becoming work and they recollect that they like sex. The body reacts with a surge of cerebrum synthetics and different changes that can help.

Keep in mind that there is no set point for the perfect measure of sex in a marriage. The appropriate measure of sex is the sum that satisfies the two accomplices.

A Prescription for a Better Sex Life

If your sexual coexistence has disappeared, it can require some investment and exertion to get it in the groove again. The best arrangement is moderately basic, however very difficult for some, couples: Start discussing sex.

Take care of business: Have sex, regardless of whether you are not in the state of mind. Sex triggers hormonal and substance reactions in the body, and regardless of whether you are not in the disposition, odds are you will arrive rapidly once you start.

Set aside a few minutes for sex: Busy accomplices regularly state they are unreasonably occupied for sex, yet strikingly, truly bustling individuals appear to discover time to have illicit relationships. The truth of the matter is, sex is useful for your relationship. Make it a need.

Talk: Ask your accomplice what the person needs. Shockingly, this is by all accounts the greatest test couples face with regards to rebooting their sexual experiences.

The initial two proposals are plain as day, however how about we set aside some effort to investigate the third step: conversing with your accomplice about sex. Dr. Hatfield of the University of Hawaii is one of the pioneers of relationship science. She built up the Passionate Love scale we investigated before in this guide. Whenever Dr. Hatfield directed a progression of meetings with people about their sexual wants, she found that people share considerably more practically speaking than they understand, they simply tend not to discuss sex with one another. Here's a straightforward exercise dependent on Dr. Hatfield's examination that could hugely affect your sexual coexistence:

Discover Two Bits of Paper and Two Pens.

Presently, plunk down with your accomplice so every one of you can record five things you need a greater amount of during sex with your accomplice. The appropriate responses shouldn't be nitty-gritty sex acts (in spite of the fact that that is fine if it is critical to you). In a perfect world, your answers should concentrate on behaviors you want - being garrulous, sentimental, delicate, trial or courageous.

If you resemble the couples in Dr. Hatfield's examination, you may find that you share undeniably more for all intents and purpose as far as sexual wants than you understand. Here are the appropriate responses Dr. Hatfield's couples gave.

How about we see what couples shared for all intents and purposes. The two accomplices needed enchantment, guidelines, and experimentation.

The fundamental difference for people is the place sexual want starts. Men needed their spouses to start sex all the more frequently and be less restrained in the room. Yet, for ladies, behavior outside the room additionally made a difference. They needed their accomplice to be hotter, useful in their lives, and they needed love and compliments both all through the room.

Remaining Faithful

People can prepare themselves to ensure their connections and raise their sentiments of responsibility.

Would you be able to Predict Infidelity?

At whatever year around 10 percent of wedded individuals — 12 percent of men and 7 percent of ladies — state they have engaged in sexual relations outside their marriage. The moderately low paces of yearly duping cover the far higher pace of lifetime conning. Among individuals, more than 60, around one out of four men and one of every seven ladies concede they have ever conned.

Various investigations in the two creatures and people recommend that there might be a hereditary part to disloyalty. While science presents a convincing defense that there is some hereditary part to tricking, we likewise realize that hereditary qualities are not fate. What's more, until there is a quick quality test to decide the betrayal danger of your accomplice, the discussion about the hereditary qualities of disloyalty isn't especially helpful to anybody.

There are some character attributes known to be related to bamboozling. A report in The Archives of Sexual Behavior found that two attributes anticipated hazard for unfaithfulness in men. Men who are effectively stimulated (called "affinity for sexual excitation") and men who are excessively worried about sexual execution disappointment are bound to swindle. The discovering originates from an investigation of almost 1,000 people. In the example, 23 percent of men and 19 percent of ladies announced consistently undermining an accomplice.

For ladies, the primary indicators of unfaithfulness were relationship bliss (ladies who are upset in their association are twice as prone to cheat) and being explicitly out-of-synchronize with their accomplice (a circumstance that makes ladies multiple times as liable to cheat as ladies who feel explicitly perfect with their accomplices).

Ensure Your Relationship

1. Plan Ahead for Temptation. People can create adapting procedures to remain devoted to an accomplice.

    A progression of unordinary studies driven by John Lydon, an analyst at McGill University in Montreal, saw how individuals in a submitted relationship respond even with allurement. In one investigation, profoundly dedicated wedded people were solicited to rate the engaging quality from individuals of the contrary sex in a progression of photographs. As anyone might expect, they gave the most noteworthy appraisals to individuals who might commonly be seen as alluring.

    Afterward, they were demonstrated comparable pictures and told that the individual was keen on gathering them. In that circumstance, members reliably gave those photos lower scores than they had the first run through around.

When they were pulled in to somebody who may undermine the relationship, they appeared to intuitively let themselves know, "He's not all that good." "The more dedicated you are," Dr. Lydon stated, "the less alluring you discover other individuals who undermine your relationship."

Other McGill concentrates affirmed differences in how people respond to such dangers. In one, alluring entertainers or on-screen characters were acquired to play with study members in a lounge area. Afterward, the members were posed inquiries about their connections, especially how they would react to an accomplice's awful behavior, such as being late and neglecting to call.

Men who had quite recently been being a tease were less lenient of the theoretical terrible behavior, recommending that the alluring entertainer had immediately worn down their responsibility. In any case, ladies who had been being a tease were bound to pardon and to rationalize the man, recommending that their prior being a tease had set off a defensive reaction when examining their relationship.

"We figure the men in these examinations may have had responsibility, however, the ladies had the emergency course of action — the appealing elective sets off the alert," Dr. Lydon said. "Ladies certainly code that as a danger. Men don't."

The investigation likewise took a gander at whether an individual can be prepared to oppose enticement. The group provoked male understudies who were in dedicated dating connections to envision running into an alluring lady on an end of the week when their sweethearts were away. A portion of the men were then approached to build up an alternate course of action by filling in the sentence "When she approaches me, I will _____ to secure my relationship."

Since the specialists morally couldn't acquire a genuine lady to go about as an enticement, they made a computer-generated simulation game in which two out of four rooms included subliminal pictures of an alluring lady. A large portion of the men who had worked on opposing enticement avoided the rooms with alluring ladies; however, among men who had not polished obstruction, two out of three inclined toward the allurement room.

Obviously, it is a lab study and doesn't generally disclose to us what may occur in reality with a genuine lady or man enticing you to stray from your relationship. Be that as it may, if you stress you may be defenseless against allurement on an excursion for work, practice obstruction by reminding yourself the means you will take to keep away from enticement and ensure your relationship.

2. Keep Your Relationship Interesting. Researchers hypothesize that your degree of duty may rely upon how much an accomplice improves your life and expands your perspectives — an idea that Dr. Aron, the Stony Brook brain science educator, calls "self-extension."

To quantify this quality, couples are posed a progression of inquiries: How much does your accomplice give a wellspring of energizing encounters? What amount has realizing your accomplice made you a superior individual? What amount do you consider your to be as an approach to grow your very own abilities?

The Stony Brook specialists directed tests utilizing exercises that animated self-development. A few couples were given ordinary errands, while others participated in a senseless exercise where they were integrated and requested to creep on mats, driving forth chamber with their heads. The investigation was fixed so the couples bombed as far as possible on the initial two attempts, yet scarcely made it on the third, bringing about much festival.

Couples were given relationship tests when the trial. The individuals who had partaken in the difficult action posted more noteworthy increments in adoration and relationship fulfillment than the individuals who had not experienced triumph together. The scientists estimate that couples who investigate new places and attempt new things will take advantage of sentiments of self-development, lifting their degree of duty.

3. Maintain a strategic distance from Opportunity. In one review, therapists at the University of Vermont asked 349 people in submitted connections about sexual dreams. Completely 98 percent of the men and 80 percent of the ladies announced having envisioned a sexual experience with somebody other than their accomplice in any event once in the past two months. The more extended couples were as one, the almost certain the two accomplices were to report such dreams.

Be that as it may, there is a major difference between fantasizing about treachery and really finishing. The most grounded hazard factor for disloyalty, analysts have discovered, exists not inside the marriage yet outside: circumstance.

For a considerable length of time, men have normally had the most chances to swindle on account of extended periods of time at the workplace, business travel, and authority over family funds. Be that as it may, today, the two people spend late hours at the workplace and travel on business. Furthermore, notwithstanding for ladies who remain at home, cellphones, email and texting have all the earmarks of being enabling them to frame increasingly hint connections outside of their relationships. Subsequently, your most obvious opportunity at devotion is to constrain openings that may enable you to stray. Submitted people keep away from circumstances that could prompt terrible choices - like lodging bars and late evenings with associates.

4. Picture Your Beloved. We as a whole realize that occasionally the more you attempt to oppose something - like dessert or a cigarette - the more you desire it. Relationship specialists state a similar guideline can impact an individual who sees a man or lady who is keen on them. The more you consider opposing the individual, the more enticing the person moves toward becoming. Instead of letting yourself know "Be great. Oppose," the better procedure is to begin considering the individual you cherish, the amount they intend to you and what they add to your life. Concentrate on adoring contemplations and the delight of your family, not sexual want for your mate -

the objective here is to clammy down the sex drive, not wake it up.

Chapter 3 – Habit Stacking

What is Habit Stacking?

Humanity should not act morally right only because it is to the overall advantage of society. The reason for this is because morals form an essential aspect of maintaining the identity of individuals living in a community. There is a close relationship between personal development and morality, with psychologists in the present-day considering morality to correspondingly change with personal development. The mannerisms and behaviors of individuals within society depend on their ability to act morally right.

Renowned psychologists such as Jean Piaget, Elliot Turiel and Lawrence Kohlberg state that morality develops through cognitive stages in the life of an individual. The reason for this is because the individual accesses different levels of information as they grow up, maturing and becoming more intelligent. The need to act in a moral manner, consequently, should not be for the benefit of the overall community, but for the development stages in the individual, as well. Morality in an individual keeps developing as long as they interact with others in society, and this is crucial in determining their behaviors and attitudes.

People should not just act in a moral manner just for the benefit of society because it has a significant influence on an individual's moral self-image. Members of the community always attempt to act in a moral manner because of a sense of responsibility and collectiveness. Maintaining a good moral self-image has an influence on the behavior of an individual because it either makes them confident or deprives them of it. Confidence in the self-image of an individual has an impact on the manner in which they will socialize with the rest of the community.

There is a very close relationship between morality and religion in society. People should not choose to act in a moral manner simply because it is to the overall advantage of society. Religious teachings show that morality should be the fabric of every community living in the world because good behavior brings human beings closer to God. Setting a good example from an individual sense creates awareness for all the members of the community. All religions emphasize the fact that the persona of God is that of a Holy One, and human beings should always try to replicate this as they were made in His likeness.

Religions have proven to be critical in dealing with different moral dilemmas that plague society. Hinduism, for instance, specifies that killing is wrong, but there are circumstances in life where it might be justified. Such justifications are made possible because of a wider understanding of religion, despite the fact that there is no synonymy between religion and morality. The life of every individual must be considered when making crucial decisions, and that is the reason why religions such as Hinduism recognize the individual over the entire community when necessary.

This is yet more evidence of the fact that people should not act morally right just for the sake of the benefit of the community. Their own ability to live and interact with everybody else in the world will depend on their ability to develop moral behaviors. Religious and morality value systems only co-exist because the principles offer a reflection of the manner in which humanity should conduct their lives. Contemporary secular frameworks such as humanism and free thought also exhibit signs of synonymy with religion. The reason for this is because they emphasize that society can only progress through the faith and contribution of each individual.

People should also not just consider acting morally just for the overall benefit of society because human progress and freedom depend on it. Several people in the world desire to truly be free from any system that weighs down their lives, but the definition of freedom is sometimes confusing. According to the philosopher Immanuel Kant, human beings are rational and therefore capable of true freedom. When people act freely, they are performing a duty in society because there is no inclination to their actions. This means that acting in a moral manner helps an individual develop their own understanding of the world without directly benefiting the overall community.

Moral actions provide a sense of duty in individuals that provides extra motivation towards being responsible. Morality makes people work in a coordinated manner, and this always offers the hope of a bright future. Acting in a moral manner is of benefit to an individual because it helps to create a sense of purpose in life through togetherness with other people. The experience of life becomes much more exciting and tolerable when acting in a moral manner because it becomes easier to socialize and interact with other people.

Moral actions help to inspire collective progress and evolution in individuals. Change is the one constant in the world that determines how societies form and survive through times. The direct consequence is that people can only achieve true personal progress by acting in a moral manner because it brings everybody together. Civilizations and modern societies would not have been able to form through history if there was not a sense of morality in human societies. The reason for this is because acting in a moral manner provides an individual with insight into the necessity of working together to get through life.

People should not act morally only because it is to the overall advantage of society as true happiness is determined by moral actions. Psychologists suggest that moral acts such as kindness and faithfulness create a sense of peace and belonging in individuals. True happiness in life can only be achieved through love, and this inspires an individual into moral actions. Moral actions offer a sense of purpose and duty, and this sense of responsibility provides genuine happiness in the life of an individual. The direct benefit for the community is obvious because such individuals are able to interact very well with the community, but performing moral actions also provides a sense of exhilaration about living life.

I believe that I have good moral character because my idea of integrity is based on kindness, mutual respect, and love. A person of high integrity, according to me, is one who is ready to help others out and display a high level of kindness even though they are not getting rewarded for their efforts. Similarly, an individual who can respect not only the people around them, but the natural environment, as well, then such an individual is worthy of high integrity according to me.

The virtues that I practice are temperance and justice because I believe that we should treat ourselves as well as others in a respectful manner. I believe that affirming the status of justice in society is important, and this results in the temperance among the population that is good for productivity. The virtues that I aspire to practice are courage and prudence; courage refers to the inner bravery to take up difficult challenges without quitting. Prudence refers to the act of being cautious, and this reflects on my renewed interest to always research and seek knowledge before making decisions.

The ethical theory that I try to follow is Kant's Ethics Theory that emphasizes moral actions are characterized by whether they fulfill the individual's responsibilities/duty. According to the theory, the decision between right and wrong is determined by whether the specific action fulfilled a pre-determined duty. Therefore, the overall consequence of the action does not determine whether it is right or wrong, and being good is determined by moral law that applies to everybody regardless of their interests. Therefore, this ethical theory emphasizes the need to treat everybody equally in society as a measure of being good and morally upstanding in society.

I believe that ethics plays a very important role in my life because it would not be possible for me to be happy without trying to be ethical. Ethics is not just about the individual, but it is about their interactions with the rest of the community and how they contribute towards general progress. Being ethical means that the individual is productive because they are able to contribute respectfully and happily towards the development and advancement of the community. I know that I would be unhappy if I tried living without trying to be ethical because everybody else would also be treating me badly.

I value ethics in my life also because it allows me to grow as an individual morally and spiritually. When an individual behaves in an ethical manner, they are able to learn more about their community and interact with an increasing number of people. By being ethical, I am able to achieve my objectives with ease because I can interact with different people as well as institutions with success. Being ethical is directly responsible for me progressing my understanding of society and how best to contribute to the advancements.

Ethics has provided me with a set of moral codes from which offer suitable guidance for every action I take. As a result of my understanding and value for ethics, I am able to conduct different activities and manage my behavior in a respectful manner. An ethical approach to life has allowed me to develop my character and respect for other people in society. I am able to make friends from all spheres of life, and I attribute this to valuing ethics highly in my life as it plays an increasingly important role in influencing my life now and in the future.

How to Apply Habit Stacking to Your Life

Habits are a ground-breaking approach to make positive changes in your life. The test is including new habits and bringing an end to unfortunate propensities.

Be that as it may, you can stack the habit deck to support you. All the more unequivocally, you can structure yourself for progress by stacking habits, or habit stacking. Habit stacking is just connecting together a chain of little activities into a daily schedule, where the entirety of the entire is more than the parts.

Build up the Habit of Following the Routine

The way to habit stacking is to manufacture the habit of playing out everyday practice. The routine should consolidate the habits into a straightforward stream that you can perform. Reiteration will enable you to fabricate the habits. Generally, it is about recurrence and stream.

The way to habit stacking is to adhere to the daily schedule rather than individual habits. You need to naturally spill out of one activity directly into the following activity without pondering every individual part. That is the reason it is imperative to build up the habit of following the daily schedule.

When you are ready to play out the habits without breaks or faltering, that is the point at which you realize you have manufactured an amazing habit stacking custom.

Here are the 8 stages for structure a habit stacking schedule;

1. **Pick a Time and Location.**
    Construct a daily schedule around a specific area, time of day or a mix of both.

2. **Construct One Routine at once.**
    Concentrate on each daily schedule in turn since it decreases the measure of consumption of your resolve. It is suggested that you center around one new daily practice for a month before rolling out any improvements or increments.

3. **Start with "Little Wins".**
    Look crosswise over territories in your life where little successes would pay you back. The 7 classes of habits are:

    - Connections
    - Recreation.
    - Association
    - Profitability
    - Funds
    - Wellbeing/physical wellness
    - Otherworldliness/prosperity

4. **Make a Logical Checklist.**
    Make a basic agenda of your habits and activities required to achieve each habit. It is suggested that the habits should cooperate and stream flawlessly. It is likewise suggested that your agenda of habits reflect moving starting with one room then onto the next to keep the advancement streaming.

5. **Have a "Motivation behind why".**

Have a valid justification for why behind every individual activity with the goal that you don't stop. A few people receive habit stacking procedures to enable them to live more, while others embrace them to invest more energy with their families.

6. **Be Accountable.**

It is constantly simpler to do nothing than to make a move. Refreshing individuals on our advancement to enable you to stay with it. For instance, Scott attempted a scale that tweets his weight.

Be that as it may, another approach to remain responsible is to structure it. Having a caution on your telephone to trigger you to begin to utilize your schedule every day. Attempt the Lift App on the grounds that that functions admirably.

7. **Make Small, Enjoyable Rewards.**

Reward yourself with little treats for overcoming your schedule each day for a week or month. It is prescribed that you keep the reward little and pick compensates that have a positive long haul sway, for example, a motion picture, night out, or little solid treat.

8. **Concentrate on Repetition.**

Redundancy of routine helps assemble your muscle memory. Redundancy is key for the initial 30 days of habit stacking.

Case of a Productivity Habit Stacking Routine

Set my Commodore for the main assignment. (Reason: I like to work in little squares of time.

Audit my quarterly objectives. (Reason: Reviewing three-month objectives once a day encourages me to remain concentrated on my most significant ventures.)

As should be obvious, Scott fortifies taking little activities, spilling out of one habit to the following, and having a motivation behind why so he realizes both what he's attempting to achieve and why he's doing it.

Identify my three most significant undertakings. (Reason: While I have a long venture rundown of everything that should be finished during the week, I like to concentrate on achieving a couple of real 'wins' for every day.)

Guide out the activity steps and specific achievements for each undertaking. (Reason: I should be exact with the most significant errands. Rather than recording an unclear explanation, for example, 'take a shot at next book,' I record the specific outcomes I'd like to accomplish.)

Start on the most upsetting errand. (Reason: As we've examined, when you center around the hardest undertaking first, the remainder of the day doesn't appear that hard. For me, that underlying errand consistently includes some type of composing.)

Research the main 100 free and paid books in the Kindle showcase. (Reason: From a business point of view, it is imperative to monitor what's as of now selling in my market.)

Specifically, I write in 25-to 50-minute squares, utilizing a modified adaptation of the Commodore Techniques. This is one more way I can remain concentrated on the job that needs to be done.)

Clear my work area. (Reason: I like to begin working with a sorted out work area. At last that encourages me to remain concentrated on specific undertakings and not get diverted.)

Managing Habit Stacking Disruptions and Challenges

Mishaps, slipups, diversions, and interruptions will occur. The inquiry is, what will you do about it? In any case, a superior inquiry is, in what manner will rapidly refocus when you have to?

You have to realize both how to manage interruptions and how to refocus.

There are a couple of key procedures to enable you to manage interruptions and to refocus:

Procedure 1: Reduce Overall Expectations. An excessive amount of weight on yourself can cause a negative response. Rather, center on the base, however, centers around the habits that are generally significant.

Procedure 2: Have an If-Then Plan. Interruptions occur. Your responsibility is to make an arrangement for when those triggers happen. Acknowledge that interruptions occur and don't get debilitated. He additionally says to rapidly excuse yourself and proceed onward so you can refocus.

Procedure 3: Start Small (Again). Beginning once again can be disheartening, however, that is the stuff to succeed. Searching for little successes and focus on adhering to your daily practice as opposed to concentrating on the length of the daily practice. You can include more habits after you have a firm handle on your daily schedule.

Procedure 4: Know Your Triggers. To make an If-Then Plan you have to know your triggers. Your triggers are the diversions and unfortunate propensities that take you off track or where you goof. Monitoring your negative habits to enable you to build up your daily practice.

The Benefits of Habit Stacking

Exercise, reflection, feast preparing, journaling, and perusing. What do these things share practically speaking? They are little habits that I've embraced to enable me to be progressively beneficial, vivacious, and spurred.

My mornings incorporate time for reflection, smart dieting, and care, yet it wasn't constantly similar to this.

Everything began when I chose to practice before anything else. This implied I needed to turn into a morning individual.

Following a little while, practicing in the first part of the day turned into a habit that set the foundation for different habits: I began settling on better decisions about my nourishment, I started supper preparing, started drinking more water.

I stacked one habit after another.

What Is Habit-Stacking?

Habit-stacking means building one habit and stacking another habit on top. The new habit can be digressively related, or it very well may be a totally different habit that you need to create. The thought is that you start little and stack one habit after another.

Adjusting YOUR ROUTINE:

Organizing your morning schedule helps set the pace for the remainder of the day: It enables you to get into the correct mentality, gather speed toward a superior day, and improves your general personal satisfaction. Research demonstrates that morning individuals are increasingly proactive in their lives. As indicated by the Journal of Applied Social Psychology, individuals who will, in general, get up right on time around a similar time on weekdays and ends of the week have a more prominent "capacity to make a move to change a circumstance to further one's potential benefit."

How Habit-Stacking Works

1. Identify a habit you need to create and be specific about your activity:

    With regards to building up a habit, abstain from being dubious about what you are wanting to achieve. For instance, rather than saying, "I need to peruse a book each month," record your habit in an increasingly solid manner, "I need to peruse for 20 minutes every day." Or "I need to peruse for an hour on Sunday morning." You may have an objective as a primary concern, yet making it a habit can enable you to reach, or even outperform your objective, and empower you to keep that habit over a more extended timeframe.

2. Locate the ideal time to finish the habit:

    Set yourself up for progress and locate a sensible time in your day to fuse your habit. For instance, I appreciate getting up ahead of schedule to work out, however, I likewise realize that a 5 a.m. boot camp session is a lot for me. I don't feel as fiery and conscious to drive my body during a time session around then, it likewise implies I need to wake up around 4:30 a.m. to get that going. Rather, I adhere to a 6 a.m. session since I'm bound to be conscious during that time, increasingly slanted to expand my activity and complete it.

3. Create and track your habit progress:

    Building up another habit requires some investment. Here are a couple of things you can do to remain responsible, roused, and positive while attempting to set up another habit.

    Applications: Try utilizing some habit-improvement and following applications, for example, Productive, Today, or Done. These applications help you see your improvement over the long haul, empower you to build up a streak, and make you feel cheerful after you complete a habit.

    Schedule or diary: Keeping a diary or a schedule and following how you feel are incredible approaches to consider yourself responsible and screen your advancement. Think about utilizing the Passion Planner or the Panda Planner which helps supplement and empower your habit-shaping endeavors.

    Responsibility accomplice: Identify a responsibility accomplice, either face to face, by telephone or gathering content. Set up a week by week call or meet with a companion to check in and keep tabs on your development or build up a gathering content with individuals who can keep you persuaded and help you recollect why you began.

4. When another habit is shaped, identify new habit:

A cornerstone habit is a habit that triggers other great habits. For instance, practicing is a cornerstone habit that can cause other positive examples in your life. A cornerstone habit triggers across the board change.

For example, specialists state families who eat together appear to bring up kids with better schoolwork aptitudes, higher evaluations, show more prominent passionate control, and display more certainty. The thought is that one little habit can stream down into other great habits. Practicing each day could enable you to feel less focused on, progressively vivacious, and help you eat better.

My Habit-Stacking in Effect

My morning habits have a specific reason or importance: they make me feel upbeat, give me an uplifting viewpoint in life, and set me up for progress. This is only a little depiction of how I've habit-stacked my morning.

One of my preferred things in my morning habits includes journaling or composing since I get the chance to record my aims and objectives for the afternoon.

Habit-Stacking Success Tips

There are a couple of things you can do to help with your habit advancement.

Take a stab at consistency: One awful feast doesn't make you undesirable, much the same as one plate of mixed greens doesn't make you a sound individual. It is your main event after some time that issues. If you don't do your habit one day, don't be so difficult on yourself and recollect that consistency is what's most significant in the whole deal.

Maintain a strategic distance from self-harm: You have been doing extraordinary with practicing and making sound sustenance alternatives. Try not to disrupt your endeavors by eating five cuts of pizza, a sack of chips, and a bundle of treats. Gradual advances is the way to progress when framing a habit. Start little so you don't set yourself up for disappointment.

Start now: You need to begin working out? Start fabricating your habit when you state you need to do it. Go get the running shoes, practice garments, and schedule or applications to keep you responsible and keep tabs on your development.

Approaches to Habit-Stack Your Morning

Your morning as of now comprises of habits, for example, making your bed or perusing the news. Here are some little approaches to habit stack your morning.

- Rest: Go to bed at a sensible hour and wake up simultaneously consistently without hitting the rest catch.
- Objectives: Write down three undertakings that you would like to achieve every day.
- Wellness: Exercise for at any rate of 30 minutes every day.
- Sustenance: Eat a nutritious breakfast.

These habits can help guarantee you are well-refreshed, stimulated, less pushed, and prepared to handle every day with the correct attitude and reason.

Chapter 4 – Self-Discipline

What is Self-Discipline?

Self-control shows up in different structures, for example, constancy, limitation, perseverance, thinking before acting, completing what you start doing, and has the capacity to do one's choices and plans, disregarding burden, hardships, or deterrents.

Self-restraint likewise implies discretion, the capacity to dodge unfortunate abundance of anything that could prompt negative results.

One of the primary attributes of self-control is the capacity to swear off moment and prompt gratification and delight, for some more noteworthy addition or all the more fulfilling outcomes, regardless of whether this requires exertion and time.

The term self-control frequently causes some distress and obstruction, because of the incorrect thought that it is something terrible, difficult to accomplish, and which requires a great deal of exertion and sacrifice. All things considered, practicing and accomplishing self-restraint can be fun, doesn't require strenuous endeavors, and the advantages are extraordinary.

Genuine self-control is definitely not a correctional or prohibitive lifestyle as certain individuals might suspect, and it has nothing to do with being extremist or living like a fakir. It is the statement of inward quality and backbone, crucial for managing the undertakings of everyday life and for the accomplishing of objectives.

Self-control, together with determination, can enable you to beat apathy, dawdling, and uncertainty. These aptitudes make it conceivable to make a move and drive forward with it, regardless of whether the activity is upsetting and requires exertion.

Self-restraint empowers you to practice balance in what you do, become progressively persistent, tolerant, understanding and kind. Likewise, it causes you to withstand outer weight and impact.

A self-taught individual is progressively dependable and puts additional time and exertion in what the individual does.

A self-trained individual is bound to assume responsibility for their life, set objectives, and find a way to accomplish them.

Self-restraint is very much depicted in the anecdote about the hare and the turtle, who directed a race between themselves.

The bunny realized that he was quicker, so he enabled himself to sleep in the race. At the same time, the turtle trudged along, yet with resolution and self-control, it in the long run figured out how to arrive first to the end goal.

Like the turtle, with self-control, you can complete what you start.

Here are a couple of statements about this significant point:

Self-restraint starts with the authority of your considerations. If you don't control what you figure, you can't control what you do. Just, self-restraint empowers you to think first and act a while later.

Order truly implies our capacity to get ourselves to do things when we don't need it.

Self-restraint is a type of opportunity. Opportunity from sluggishness and laziness, opportunity from the desires and requests of others, opportunity from shortcoming and dread and uncertainty. Self-restraint enables a pitcher to feel his distinction, his inward quality, his ability. He is ace of, instead of a captive to, his contemplations and feelings.

For quite a while, we are gone up against various choices. An abnormal state of discretion enables us to meet the choice that is most helpful over the long haul. This capacity causes us to withstand the enticement of picking the most agreeable or pleasurable choice. Deciding on the most effortless arrangement may be very appealing, yet just for a brief span. At the point when seen from a long haul viewpoint, all things considered, none of these "agreeable choices" add to your prosperity.

The peril lies in that that joy situated choices ordinarily don't in a split second negatively affect your life when taken independently. Whenever joined, be that as it may, the aggregate of all these unbeneficial small scale choices will shape your life and will, at last, decide your fate.

- The Definition of Self-Discipline
- The capacity to prepare and control one's direct.
- The capacity to do the things that should be finished.
- The capacity to control one's emotions and wants.

The thing self-control portrays the vital mental quality that is required to control one's behaviors, emotions and wants. If one is self-restrained, it demonstrates that one's emotions and wants are leveled out. It additionally demonstrates that one can rouse oneself to handle the assignments and issues that should be tended to. If you have an abnormal state of self-restraint, you will not avoid difficulties and obstructions that hinder you.

An Explanation of Self-Discipline

Self-control portrays not just the fundamental resolve required to do what should be finished. It likewise characterizes the capacity to withstand enticements so as to achieve long haul objectives. Essentially, it is your capacity to disregard everything that doesn't add to the achievement of your destinations. This incorporates contemplations, emotions, and enticements. Indeed, self-restraint encourages you to withstand the enticement of distractive exercises.

Despite the fact that we as a whole battle to be taught enough to complete disagreeable things, there are individuals who are more responsible for themselves than others. We should examine a portion of the primary driver why individuals battle to ace poise:

The Reasons for a Lack of Self-Discipline

The significant motivation behind why the vast majority battle to act naturally taught lies in a misperception of the fundamental idea. Most people misconstrue what poise really implies. These individuals partner self-restraint with something excruciating or over the top. They wish that being trained is simple and pleasurable. Consequently, at whatever point these people attempt to be progressively trained, it ends up being a battle that just feels not appropriate to them. They don't care for it by any means, which is the reason they rapidly come back to their usual range of familiarity.

Here's the significant viewpoint these people don't think about with regards to self-control:

The sole reason for the control idea is to cause you to get things done, regardless of if it is pleasurable or not.

Hence, the expectation behind self-restraint isn't to give you joy and euphoria. Its lone target is to enable you to achieve your long haul objectives. In any case, for what reason would it be advisable for you to develop something that doesn't give you happiness? The purpose behind this is basic. Every one of your endeavors and torments are remunerated once you make your fantasies materialize. Also, this is simply the genuine motivation behind why being a taught individual is so advantageous. It may not generally feel good when you compel yourself to remain trained, in any case, your reward will remunerate you.

What Is Self-Restraint?

Restraint manifests itself in a wide range of structures

This is what you can do if you are battling with self-control.

As a matter of first importance, attempt to evacuate the desire that one day you may really like being restrained. Much of the time, you will not. Be that as it may, if you are not anticipating that things should be simple, you'll be bound to proceed with the quest for being taught. Truth be told, when you anticipate that things should be difficult, you'll have the option to all the more likely manage the battles you experience.

Furthermore, it is significant that you consistently drive yourself to keep up discretion. Doing so will assist you in establishing the habit of being restrained. Not exclusively will this habit affect significant aspects of your life; however, it will likewise enable you to expand your odds to succeed.

Here are some more reasons why individuals need poise:

- Self-control isn't characteristic. It should be created, fortified, and worked out. In any case, the vast majority think that it is difficult to do as such. If you don't have the foggiest idea of how to successfully fabricate and fortify poise, it is genuinely difficult to create it in any case.

- A misinterpretation of discretion. Numerous erroneously see self-control as something that is prohibitive and difficult. They consider it to be habitual and are hesitant to reinforce it.

- Acknowledgment of disappointment can likewise add to an absence of discretion. At the point when individuals can live with the possibility of fizzling, it'll be difficult to keep up self-restraint.

- Enticements. We as a whole are faced with different sorts of allurements every day. Surrendering to these allurements takes after the section of an endless loop. If you don't have the essential resolution to withstand these enticements, it'll be considerably progressively difficult to bring an end to the negative habit.

- Absence of direction. An individual who does not have a genuine vision for life will discover it increasingly difficult to look after order. In any case, if you have a mission that you need to see acknowledged, you'll be bound to have the essential self-control to seek after it.

How about we proceed with the following point that will assist us with furthering comprehend what self-control is.

Benefits of Self-Discipline

Self-restraint Benefits

Self-restraint is one of the most significant and helpful abilities everybody ought to have. This ability is fundamental in each everyday issue, and however, the vast majority recognize its significance, not many plan something for fortifying it.

In spite of regular conviction, self-control doesn't mean being brutal toward yourself or carrying on with a constrained, prohibitive lifestyle. Self-control implies restraint, which is an indication of inward quality and control of yourself, your activities, and your responses.

Self-control enables you to adhere to your choices and finish them, without altering your perspective and is in this way, one of the significant necessities for accomplishing objectives.

The ownership of this ability empowers you to endure with your choices and plans until you achieve them. It additionally manifests as internal quality, helping you to beat addictions, stalling, and apathy, and to finish whatever you do.

Develop Willpower and Self Discipline

Start Building Your Willpower and Self Discipline

Direction and activities for structure up resolve and self-restraint, conquering tarrying, and sluggishness, picking up conclusiveness and persistence, and assuming responsibility for your life.

Develop Your Willpower and Self-Discipline

One of its principal attributes is the capacity to dismiss moment gratification and delight, for some more noteworthy increase, which requires investing exertion and energy to get it.

Self-control is one of the significant elements of accomplishment. It conveys what needs be in an assortment of ways:

Persistence.

The capacity not to surrender, in spite of disappointment and misfortunes.

restraint.

The capacity to oppose diversions or enticements.

Attempting on and on, until you achieve what you set out to do.

Life puts difficulties and issues on the way to progress and accomplishment, and so as to transcend them, you need to act with diligence and perseverance, and this obviously, requires self-restraint.

The ownership of this aptitude prompts self-assurance and confidence, and thus, to joy and fulfillment.

Then again, the absence of self-restraint prompts disappointment, misfortune, wellbeing and connections' issues, weight, and different issues.

This expertise is likewise valuable for beating dietary problems, addictions, smoking, drinking and negative habits. You likewise need it to cause yourself to sit and consider, practice your body, grow new aptitudes, and for personal development, profound development and reflection.

As said before, the vast majority recognize the significance and advantages of self-control, yet not many find a way to create and reinforce it. In any case, you can reinforce this capacity like some other aptitude. This is done through preparing and activities, which can discover at this site.

Self-Restraint Benefits and Importance

Self-restraint encourages you:

- Keep taking a shot at a venture, even after the underlying surge of eagerness has blurred away.
- Get up promptly toward the beginning of the day.
- Think normally.
- Abstain from acting thoughtlessly and on motivation.
- Satisfy guarantees you make to yourself and to other people.
- Keep taking a shot at your eating routine, and opposing the enticement of eating swelling sustenance's.
- Conquer the habit of observing a lot of TV.
- Defeat apathy and hesitation.
- Start perusing a book, and read it to the last page.

It will be simpler for you to reinforce your self-restraint if you:

Attempt to act and carry on as indicated by the choices you make, paying little respect to sluggishness, the inclination to tarry, or the craving to surrender and stop what you are doing.

Comprehend its significance in your life.

You can fortify your self-devotion regardless of whether it is as of now frail, with the assistance of uncommon basic activities, which you can rehearse whenever or place.

Become mindful of your undisciplined behavior and its outcomes. At the point when this mindfulness builds, you will be increasingly persuaded of the need to roll out an improvement in your life.

How Self-Discipline Can Improve Your Life

No close to home achievement, accomplishment, or objective, can be acknowledged without self-control. It is uniquely the most significant credit expected to accomplish any kind of close to home magnificence, athletic brilliance, virtuosity in expressions of the human experience, or generally remarkable execution.

What Is Self-Control?

It is the capacity to control one's driving forces, feelings, wants and behavior. It is having the option to turn down quick joy and moment gratification for picking up the long haul fulfillment and satisfaction from accomplishing higher and progressively significant objectives.

To have self-restraint is to have the option to settle on the choices, take the activities, and execute your strategy paying little respect to the deterrents, inconvenience, or difficulties, that may come your direction.

Unquestionably, being disciplined doesn't mean living a constraining or a prohibitive lifestyle. Nor, doesn't mean quitting any pretense of all that you appreciate, or, to give up fun and unwinding. It means figuring out how to concentrate your brain and energies on your objectives and endure until they are practiced. It likewise means developing an outlook whereby you are led by your conscious decisions as opposed to by your feelings, negative behavior patterns, or the influence of others. Self-restraint enables you to arrive at your objectives in a sensible time span and to live an all the more precise and fulfilling life.

The Most Effective Method to Develop Self-Discipline

Start with gradual steps. No procedure happens medium-term. Similarly, as it requires some investment to manufacture muscle, so does it set aside some effort to create self-control. The more you train and fabricate it, the more grounded you become. In exercise, if you attempt to do a lot on the double, you could harm yourself and have difficulty. In like manner, approach it slowly and carefully in structure self-control. Along these lines, start by settling on the choice to go ahead and realizing the stuff to arrive.

Realize what rouses you and what your awful triggers are. You can start by finding out about yourself! At times it is difficult to ward off desires and longings, so know the regions where your opposition is low and how to maintain a strategic distance from those circumstances. If you realize you can't avoid cake, fries, or different allurements - avoid them. Try not to have them around to bait you in snapshots of shortcoming. discipline If you additionally realize that putting weight on yourself doesn't work for you, at that point set yourself up in a domain that supports the structure of self-restraint as opposed to one that subverts it. Expel the allurements and encircle yourself with relieving and empowering things, for example, inspiring mottos and pictures of what you need to accomplish.

Realize additionally what empowers and propels you. Your self-control can go here and there with your vitality levels so play vigorous music to liven you up, move around, chuckle. Train yourself to appreciate what you are doing by being invigorated. This will make it simpler to actualize attractive and fitting behaviors into your daily schedule - which is truly what self-control is about.

Make certain behaviors a daily schedule. When you have chosen what's critical to you and which objectives to take a stab at, set up a day by day schedule that will enable you to accomplish them. For instance, if you need to eat soundly or get in shape; take steps to eat a few servings of foods grown from the ground every day and exercise for at any rate thirty minutes. Make it part of your day by day schedule and part of your self-control building. In like manner, dispose of a portion of your awful, reckless habits, whatever they might be. They can place you in a negative temper and impede your self-restraint. A poor frame of mind can likewise be an unfortunate habit.

Practice discipline. Figure out how to disapprove of a portion of your emotions, motivations, and desires. Train yourself to do what you know to be correct, regardless of whether you don't want to do it. Skip dessert a few nighttimes. Utmost your TV viewing. Fight the temptation to holler at somebody who has bothered you. Stop and think before you act. Consider results. When you practice patience, it encourages you to build up the habit of monitoring different things.

Take part in games or exercises. Sports are a great method to upgrade self-control. They train you to set objectives, center your psychological and emotional energies, become physically fit, and to coexist well with others. Taking an interest in games gives a circumstance where you figure out how to buckle down and endeavor to give a valiant effort, which thus, instructs you to incorporate the equivalent points of view and disciplines into your regular day to day existence.

Figuring out how to play a melodic instrument can be another extraordinary method to rehearse self-control. The center, reiteration, and application required in figuring out how to play an instrument is significant. Accomplishing self-restraint in any one aspect of your life reinvents your brain to pick what is correct, as opposed to what is simple.

Get motivation from those you appreciate. Michael Jordan has constantly kept up that his enormity as a ballplayer came as much from his readiness to buckle down at his art, as it did his ability. It was his longing through discipline and center that made him extraordinary compared to other ballplayers. If it worked for him, it could absolutely work for all of us.

Imagine the prizes. There is nothing more gratifying than achieving your objectives. Practice the system that high achievers and top competitors do. Undertaking yourself later on. Picture your ideal result. Feel how compensating it is and the incalculable advantages you will appreciate. Remind yourself the stuff to arrive.

The Benefits

It helps manufacture self-assurance.

You achieve more and are along these lines increasingly gainful.

You can keep up a higher resilience for dissatisfaction, deterrents and negative feelings.

Enables you to get better wellbeing, better funds, and a decent hard-working attitude.

You can arrive at your most difficult objectives all the more productively.

The more disciplined you become, the simpler life gets.

If we are to be experts in our own predetermination, we should create self-control and discretion. By concentrating on long haul benefits rather than transient inconvenience, we can urge ourselves to create of self-restraint. At last, our wellbeing and satisfaction rely upon it.

Fundamentals of Self-Discipline

Commitment

It is your degree of pledge to what you are doing that will choose your degree of accomplishment in it. Unfortunately, a great many people simply stop after the 'wish' part and scarcely take the torment to focus on their fantasies. Presumably, that is the thing that stops them to be fruitful in any undertaking.

We should get this straight that there is no alternate route to progress. The best way to be effective is to take the long street and pursue your interest with a hundred percent devotion and promise to it.

Notwithstanding, the way to progress isn't simple as it sounds to be. You need to make a few responsibilities to yourself to reach there and carry on with the life you have imagined in your fantasies.

Try not to give your tasks a chance to run your life. Coming up next are the seven responsibilities that one must make to himself on his interest in progress:

#1 Commitment: Taking huge activity regular

Since you comprehend what you need to seek after in life, it is an ideal opportunity to make an activity arrangement for it. Regardless of whether your objectives are little or huge, you should be subscribed to make gigantic moves each and every day for no reason.

It begins with setting up your mind to enthusiastically pursue your fantasies or whatever you are energetic about in life. You can start by making an arrangement. All things considered, there are many arranging instruments out there to enable you to out. While making your activity arrangement, ensure you redo it according to your needs and qualities.

Try not to be excessively easygoing or excessively yearning about them. Be as reasonable as could be expected under the circumstances so you are propelled enough to make a monstrous move on them regularly for no reason.

#2 Commitment: Never surrender.

As platitude' as it might sound yet never abandoning yourself is a definitive mantra to progress. As you stroll through life, you will tumble down ordinarily. You may likewise commit errors and fizzle, and it is completely alright. Such is reality and things will occur yet never let this hamper your spirits in any capacity.

Remember that so as to succeed and turn into your best form, you must have a great deal of confidence in yourself. This unyielding soul will enable you to overcome these extreme occasions a piece effectively. Try not to surrender ever — no matter what.

#3 Commitment: Being versatile and adapting constantly

Versatility and energy to develop can take you puts in life. It is dismal to see that individuals are excessively inflexible in their musings and convictions that they dismiss any proposals or new approach given to them. It very well may be perilous for their vocation and by and large life all in all.

In the expressions of Charles Darwin, "It isn't the most grounded of the species that endure, nor the most shrewd that endures. The one is the most versatile to change."

Learn as much as you can from whosoever you need as it would be something nobody can detract from you. Learn constantly as most occasions there is more than one approach to do an equivalent thing. The minute you shed your assumptions and grasp versatility, openings will consequently introduce themselves in the most unforeseen ways.

#4 Commitment: Not doing exploitative or shameless stuff

There are two different ways to succeed: the easy way and difficult one. Going for a simple way means doing 'whatever' it takes to reach there — by snare or by hoodlum. It means taking easy routes, favors, doing dishonest things that conflict with the ethical compass. Presently, the dedication isn't to do any of the things referenced previously.

You may get allured with accomplishing something unscrupulous and get snappy outcomes. Nonetheless, such things consistently accompany a cost — that can without much of a stretch ruin everything inside a snap of a finger. Keep in mind that the voyage to progress is going to test your character alongside devotion.

#5 Commitment: Believing in yourself

You must have confidence in yourself before others start putting stock in you. Whatever is that you might want to accomplish, ensure that you have confidence in it and trust your capacities to achieve it.

The issue is that individuals will, in general, think little of the capacities that prevent them to arrive at their actual potential. Take a journal and compose your qualities, uniqueness, most prominent accomplishments, and achievements in it and read them so anyone might hear each morning. This little system can do marvels to fortify your confidence in yourself.

Ordinary, I see such huge numbers of individuals with a great deal of potential however their low confidence and absence of certainty are impeding them to progress. It is basic to acknowledge yourself and put stock in capacities to carry on with your best life.

#6 Commitment: Maintaining appropriate work-life balance

Do you realize what is the absolute most significant thing in your life? It is nothing else except for your wellbeing. Your physical and psychological wellness has a significant influence on your life as everything legitimately or in a roundabout way relies upon it.

Try not to get too expended in buckling down that you start disregarding your wellbeing. If you have worked enthusiastically for straight 40 hours, it bodes well to give your body the rest it merits. If you are taking a shot at ends of the week, take a stab at spending, in any event, a couple of hours with your precious ones and energize your batteries.

#7 Commitment: Willingness to lose some rest and saying NO

Achievement regularly goes to the individuals who are happy to take the necessary steps to be effective. You would need to work your butt off as well as might need to disapprove of a few things that don't line up with your objectives.

It may entice to go out to shop or gathering with companions on ends of the week yet chipping away at your startup or composing your next blog is what is going to have to make a real effect. If you are taking a shot at your particular employment during the day then the best way to take a shot at your fantasy is by losing some rest.

One more thing, start saying NO more regularly. It may take a great deal of mental fortitude to disapprove of companions however doing it will make your life more fruitful and more joyful than theirs.

The thing about duty is that it means remaining faithful to what you said you would do long after the disposition you said it in has left you. Presently, it is up to you might want to submit yourself and follow up on things or let them transpire.

Optimization

A caffeinated drink promotion at present airing asks, "Imagine a scenario where individuals had a battery-level symbol, as on your telephone?" as we see an arrangement of individuals dressed for the workplace, exploring a city walkway, each with their own rate level, most green, some red and running out. "You'd see a great deal of us strolling around," the voice-over proceeds, "needing a revive." The drink is then exhibited as a sort of extremely quick charging link for the body.

The promotion's trick plays not exclusively to the dream that our life power can be caught in some straightforward unidimensional measure and effectively oversaw yet in addition to the more extensive, progressively guileful thought that individuals should capacity like telephones. The desires we have for our gadgets soak our desires for other people (regardless of whether they are companions, family, administration laborers, or robots) and at last ourselves. We ought to be fit for dealing with any assignment we're enlisted for, moving flawlessly starting with one interface then onto the next, starting with one application then onto the next, for whatever length of time that required. If we can't, we have to "revive" ourselves: to locate the correct medication mix or exercise routine, or else to pass on ourselves for absolutely as long as we have to return to 100 percent. The possibility that we are something besides independent and vitality autonomous is suspended for a dream of instrumental control.

Computerized systems and assets can give the figment of availability — if anybody can get to dietary rules, for example, anybody ought to have the option to tail them. This mistaken idea creates an ethical buildup: If anybody can "do it" — be sound and alluring and alarm and arranged to gain by any chance — than to not do it is an ethical coming up short. We may perceive ailment as no-flaw yet in addition rebuff any "disappointment" to treat it as indicated by social conventions.

Self-advancement turns into a type of devotion: privatized work of moral obligation as open great. This happens as a guarantee to effectiveness, as in "if you are not enhancing your life to help your work (regardless of whether that work helps anybody other than your manager) you are dead weight" — a channel on other individuals' material and enthusiastic assets. If work is life, at that point proficient objectives are good goals as well. This predicts a condition wherein wellbeing is vague from efficiency.

This week, Rebecca O'Dwyer expounds on the proliferation of temperance applications and how these work to rethink the idea. Expelled from the setting of compulsion, moderation is recast as a wellbeing practice, similar to prevailing fashion eating less junk food, and acquired line under the talk of self-advancement. By this reasoning, one can be "calm" even while consuming medications like ayahuasca or LSD to increment imaginative potential, as "moderation" is recast as a condition of availability for work.

What's in question isn't close to home wellbeing and bliss, not to mention aggregate prosperity, but instead manager requests for yield. As Alex Beattie states, "disconnectionism recodes self-care as the upkeep of a standardizing level of profitability, with internet-based life consumes fewer calories and such filling in as plain customs of control and core interest." The "advanced detox" isn't suggested to such an extent as a method for satisfaction or commitment with life yet as an administrative procedure for keeping up beneficial core interest. The defamation of diversion works as a vindication for the business cooptation of consideration.

As social backings are being destroyed and occupations are rare and frequently inadequately paid, appearing anything short of 100 percent focused on working at whatever point starts to appear to be hazardous. To release oneself is to lose critical upper hand, which is progressively conflated with a caring good and physical unfitness. As O'Dwyer brings up, the distraction some have with the details of their utilization has a superstitious cast. Fanatical self-care is simply the flipside devastation: Both can give the hallucination of authority over life's shameful acts and unusual torments, a feeling of organization — as though we generally get what we pick and what we merit.

Turning into the superhuman adaptation of yourself through eating regimen, work out, biohacking, picking up learning, and so forth and accomplishing self-enhancement is an energizing objective. In the start of your adventure towards self-streamlining, it may very well entice the need to make plenty of changes with respect to your wellbeing, wellness, and lifestyle habits on the double and to attempt to accomplish more, so you will begin to get results quicker, yet this is conceivably the quickest method to progress toward becoming overpowered. .

How would you become superhuman and arrive at self-enhancement truly? You certainly don't end up one by workaholic behavior or propelling yourself excessively hard and at last consuming yourself out.

While attempting to turn into a definitive you, it is critical to likewise deal with your emotional wellness and to permit yourself an opportunity to rest and recuperate, so you can perform ideally and perform like a superhuman when you do work or exercise.

You can be excessively determined and excessively centered around changing your wellbeing, however doing so can really harm your wellbeing at last. Making a decent attempt to turn into a solid superhuman could be what will really wind up harming your wellbeing, basically as a result of overabundance stress and uneasiness. There is no decent method to state this, however, cortisol (the primary pressure hormone) is a bitch.

If you attempt and do everything splendidly, you could make yourself stress more, and wind up hindering the procedure and your advancement. You can push hard for about fourteen days, yet then wear out and wind up taking seven days to rest, since you simply don't have the vitality.

A portion of the reactions of raised cortisol include:

Accelerating the maturing procedure by separating collagen;

Harming the safe framework, and making you bound to end up wiped out;

Setting off the creation of insulin, which can cause fat addition and increment the danger of diabetes;

State of mind changes (particularly feeling on edge, low, or effectively aggravated);

Hypertension; and

Causing the generation of more testosterone in ladies with polycystic ovarian disorder (PCOS).

Here are a couple of tips on how you can, in any case, become the superhuman rendition of you, and improve your psychological and physical execution, and accomplish self-streamlining without harming your wellbeing or sacrificing your psychological mental soundness:

Breaking Point Your Consumption of Caffeine Sources

If you can deal with having a couple of cups of espresso daily without getting to be restless, that is fine, however, if you have excessively, it can cause you to end up unsteady or on edge. When you feel on edge, you will not actually feel like a superhuman or perform like one.

Caffeine can help improve both mental and physical execution, and three cups of espresso daily should give you enough to get the advantages (that is if you can endure caffeine). A few people, similar to me, are excessively delicate to caffeine and need to remove it for the most part. The main caffeine I expend is what is found in my day by day chocolate treat that I make with cacao.

Inhale Your Way to Becoming a Superhuman

If you begin to feel overpowered by your work or the majority of the objectives that you have set for yourself, attempt to do some breathing activities. They will enable you to quiet down and remain centered. This will help decrease overpower.

You can begin by simply taking in through your eye for a couple of forgets about and for a couple. Do this for a couple of minutes and perceive how you feel. To begin with, you can put on your main tune and inhale profoundly for the term.

Ponder Your Way to Self-Optimization

This takes the entire breathing thing to the following level. By pondering, you can diminish uneasiness, remain concentrated and quiet on your superhuman and self-improvement venture, and receive the rewards that it has for your wellbeing and cerebrum. These incorporate decreasing cortisol levels, which will help fat misfortune and diminish mind haze, just as hindering maturing.

Simply reflecting for ten minutes daily is sufficient for you to begin encountering the advantages of contemplation for self-advancement.

Emotions

Have you at any point said something out of resentment that you later lamented? Do you let dread convince you not to go out on a limb that could truly profit you? If thus, you are not the only one.

The feelings are amazing. Your state of mind decides how you cooperate with individuals, how a lot of cash you spend, how you manage difficulties, and how you invest your energy.

Overseeing your feelings will enable you to turn out to be rationally more grounded. Luckily, anybody can turn out to be better at managing their feelings. Much the same as some other ability, dealing with your feelings requires practice and devotion.

Experience Uncomfortable Emotions But Don't Stay Stuck in Them

Dealing with your feelings isn't equivalent to stifling them. Disregarding your trouble or imagining you don't feel torment will not cause those feelings to leave.

Actually, unaddressed enthusiastic injuries are probably going to deteriorate after some time. Also, there is a decent shot smothering your sentiments will make you go to undesirable adapting abilities - like nourishment or liquor.

It is essential to recognize your sentiments while likewise perceiving that your feelings don't need to control you. If you wake up on an inappropriate side of the bed, you can assume responsibility for your state of mind and turn your day around. If you are irate, you can quiet yourself down.

Here are three different ways to deal with your state of mind:

1. Reframe Your Thoughts

Your feelings influence the manner in which you see occasions. If you are feeling restless and you get an email from the supervisor that says she needs to see you immediately, you may accept that you will get terminated. If in any case, you are feeling glad when you get that equivalent email, your first idea may be that you will be advanced or praised on a vocation very much done.

Consider the passionate channel you are taking a gander at the world through. At that point, reframe your considerations to build up a progressively practical view.

If you discover yourself thinking, "This systems administration occasion will be a finished exercise in futility. Nobody is going to converse with me and I'm going to resemble an imbecile," remind yourself, "It is dependent upon me to get something out of the occasion. I'll acquaint myself with new individuals and show enthusiasm for finding out about them."

At times, the simplest method to increase a different viewpoint is to make a stride back and ask yourself, "What might I say to a companion who had this issue?" Answering that question will remove a portion of the feeling from the condition so you can think all the more normally.

If you end up dwelling on negative things, you may need to change the divert in your mind. A fast physical movement, such as taking a walk or clearing off your work area, can enable you to quit ruminating.

2. Name Your Emotions

Before you can change how you believe, you have to recognize what you are encountering at the present time. It is safe to say that you are anxious? Do you feel disillusioned? It is safe to say that you are dismal?

Remember that outrage here and there covers feelings that vibe defenseless - like disgrace or humiliation. So give close consideration to what's truly going on within you.

Put a name on your feelings. Remember you may feel an entire bundle of feelings without a moment's delay - like restless, disappointed, and eager.

Marking how you feel can take a great deal of the sting out of the feeling. It can likewise help you take cautious note of how those sentiments are probably going to influence your choices.

3. Take part in a Mood Booster

When you are feeling terrible, you are probably going to take part in exercises that keep you in from that perspective. Detaching yourself, thoughtlessly looking through your telephone, or griping to individuals around you are only a couple of the ordinary "go-to terrible state of mind behaviors" you may enjoy.

In any case, those things will keep you stuck. You need to make a positive move if you need to feel much improved.

Think about the things you do when you feel cheerful. Do those things when you are feeling awful and you'll begin to feel good.

Here are a couple of instances of state of mind sponsors:

- Call a companion to discuss something charming (not to keep whining).
- Take a walk.
- Think for a couple of minutes.
- Tune in to uplifting music.

Continue Practicing Your Emotional Regulation Skills

Dealing with your feelings is intense now and again. What's more, there will probably be a specific feeling - like resentment - that occasionally bamboozles you.

Be that as it may, the additional time and consideration you spend on controlling your feelings, the rationally more grounded you'll turn into. You'll pick up trust in your capacity to deal with uneasiness while additionally realizing that you can settle on sound decisions that shift your state of mind.

Feelings are the most present, squeezing and in some cases excruciating power in our lives. We are driven step by step by our feelings. We take risks since we're energized for new prospects. We cry since we've been harmed and we make sacrifices since we cherish. No ifs, ands or buts, our feelings manage our musings, expectations, and activities with better authority than our balanced personalities. In any case, when we follow up on our feelings too rapidly, or we follow up on an inappropriate sort of feeling, we regularly settle on choices that we later regret.

Our emotions can modify hazardous limits. Veer excessively far to one side and you are verging on fury. Steer a lot to one side and you are in a condition of happiness. Similarly, as with numerous different parts of life, feelings are best met with a feeling of balance and a coherent point of view. It is not necessarily the case that we should prevent ourselves from experiencing passionate feelings for or bouncing for euphoria after extraordinary news. These really are the better things in life. It is negative feelings that must be dealt with outrageous consideration.

Negative feelings, similar to wrath, jealousy or harshness, will in general winding wild, particularly following they have been activated. In time, these sorts of feelings can develop like weeds, gradually molding the brain to work on inconvenient sentiments and ruling everyday life. Ever met an individual who's reliably irate or unfriendly? They weren't brought into the world that way. In any case, they enabled certain feelings to mix inside them for such a long time that they wound up innate sentiments emerging very every now and again.

Exercises to Improve Your Self-Discipline

What are some every day great activities to rehearse self-control?

1. **Scrub Down Every Morning**

    Cold showers suck. Driving yourself to persevere through the frigid impact of a virus shower before anything else requires discipline and a high edge for agony.

    They are difficult, they are awful, and they are not happy regardless of whether it is only for 30 seconds. Start your three day weekend by constraining yourself to persevere through intense pressure and conquer the craving for a warm and simple shower. It will be hard. In any case, it will manufacture orders like nothing else.

2. **Reflect for 10 Minutes per Day**

    Reflection may appear to be an odd method to construct discipline. All things considered, you simply need to sit on your butt and consider nothing, isn't that so? All things considered, not actually. Reflection expects you to teach your musings. To clear your brain, focus your body, and reconnect with your breath.

    Contemplation causes you to get out of the psychological mess and enables you to reconnect with yourself. What's more, it is harder than you might suspect. Sitting and pondering only your breath requires gigantic control and core interest. If you are happy to give this a go for 30 days, you will build your control and self-discipline in astonishing ways.

3. Start Your Day With 100 Push-Ups or a 1-Mile Run

100 push-ups should just take you 5 minutes. A one-mile run takes around 10 minutes. Be that as it may, they are amazing assets for structure discipline. By beginning your day with some type of physical activity, you will kick off your prosperity for the duration of the day and power yourself to accomplish something awkward and difficult before anything else.

Do this before your morning cold shower and you will have indicated more order before 8 a.m. than the vast majority do ALL day.

4. Make Your Bed

Making your bed takes 5 minutes. However, it is a little movement that requires discipline in light of the fact that there is no genuine motivation to do it. Certainly, it enables you to achieve one errand before you kick your three day weekend.

Be that as it may, dislike making your bed will expand your salary, make you progressively beneficial, or increment your sex advance. It is a definitive pointless activity. Be that as it may, you should, in any case, do it. Making your bed before anything else places you into a taught and profitable state promptly when you start your day.

It is likewise an amazing inspiration to remain wakeful as opposed to slithering into the warm sheets.

5. **Dispense with Distractions**

    Diversions murder discipline. If you need to be increasingly trained for the duration of the day, kill all diversions. Mood killer your telephone, introduce a Facebook news channel blocker, turn off notifications on your PC and spotlight just on the job that needs to be done.

    This will enable you to be progressively engaged and gainful and will require enormous measures of everyday discipline. Staying away from the dopamine-instigating internet based life notifications and instant messages isn't simple, however, it is well justified, despite all the trouble.

6. **Stop Complaining**

    Grumbling resembles malignant growth in your spirit. You have a great deal to be appreciative for. However, every time you gripe, you disclose to yourself that your life sucks and that things are not the manner in which that they ought to be (notwithstanding when they are incredible).

    So quit grumbling.

    It resembles a toxin. It occupies you from the great and makes you center around everything that isn't right. It makes other individuals like you less, makes you pass up on chances, and diverts you from carrying on with an astonishing life.

    Purchase an elastic band and put it on your correct wrist. If you end up whining for the duration of the day, move it to one side wrist. You will likely make it 30 days with that elastic band remaining on your correct hand. If you can do this, your control, satisfaction, and inspiration will soar.

Self-control and Willpower - Your Inner Strength

These two abilities are the providers of inward quality. They can enable you to transform you and change your habits. They are the most helpful abilities for everybody, in each everyday issue and for any age.

Self-restraint and resolution invigorate the internal to act, get things done, and to proceed with your activities, regardless of difficulties and impediments.

The total manual for resolve and self-control

Ask yourself the accompanying inquiries:

How frequently have you attempted to change your dietary patterns, quit smoking, or rise prior to the beginning of the day, yet you didn't have enough inward quality and ingenuity?

Do you some of the time, feel that you come up short on the internal solidarity to make a move, demonstration decisively or drive forward?

How often you have you chosen to take a walk, realizing how brilliant you feel a while later, however because of lethargy or absence of inward quality, you remained at home and stared at the TV?

Do you start getting things done, however, quit after a brief time?

Are there any habits that you need to change, however, feel that you come up short on the fundamental internal solidarity to change?

You can change this behavior when you reinforce your self-restraint and resolution. All you need is some preparation, direction, and counsel.

Subsequent to creating and reinforcing your resolve and create self-control, you will have the option to pick your responses and beat negative habits. These two abilities make you feel all the more dominant, sure, and responsible for yourself and of your life.

There is a misinterpretation in the open personality in regards to the two aptitudes we are discussing here. It is incorrectly accepted that their advancement requires a ton of mental and physical strain and exertion. This isn't valid. You can develop these abilities through basic activities, and even appreciate the procedure.

Develop Willpower and Self Discipline

Start Building Your Willpower and Self Discipline

Direction and activities for structure up resolution and self-control, conquering dawdling, and sluggishness, picking up definitiveness and tirelessness, and assuming responsibility for your life.

Develop Your Willpower and Self-Discipline

It is said that individuals with more prominent discretion are more joyful than individuals who don't have this capacity. Self-taught individuals additionally have inward quality, which causes them to bargain all the more effectively and certainly with issues and deterrents.

At the point when these two aptitudes are well-created, there is more control, more power, and more confidence, and one stands behind their choices. This implies better odds of achieving what one sets to do.

Self-restrained individuals ordinarily have more determination than others and don't enable their decisions to be directed by motivations or emotions and what other individuals state or do.

Conclusion

Thank you for making it through to the end of *Learn Habits of Highly Effective People & How to Increase Self Discipline*, let's hope it was informative and able to provide you with all of the tools you need to achieve your goals whatever they may be.

The next step is to like us on social media and put to practice what you learn from here.

Finally, if you found this book useful in any way, an honest review is always appreciated!

www.ingramcontent.com/pod-product-compliance
Lightning Source LLC
Chambersburg PA
CBHW071903070526
44583CB00016B/1821